fresh&simple

delicious meals, freshly prepared in minutes

by Myles Beaufort and Suzie Smith

PERIPLUS EDITIONS
Singapore • Hong Kong • Indonesia

Contents

Fresh and Simple Cooking 6
Cooking Methods and Tips 7
Essential Ingredients 9

Soups, Salads and Vegetables
Simple Potato and Leek Soup 10
New England Clam Chowder 12
Chunky Vegetable Soup 13
Hearty Fish Stew 14
Bean and Pasta Soup 16
Red Cabbage and Beef Borscht 17
Chinese Chicken Noodle Soup 18
French Onion Soup 19
Classic Potato Salad 20
Fresh Vinaigrette Salad Dressing 20
Oriental Chicken Salad 22
Thai Grilled Beef Salad 23
Vegetarian Pasta Salad with Olives 24
Warm Main-course Spinach Salad 25
Mediterranean Pasta Salad 26
Thai Chicken Noodle Salad 27
Fresh Potato Curry with Peas 28
Spinach and Cheese Frittata 29

Pasta
Beef Stroganoff with Egg Noodles 30
Fettuccine with Ham and Parmesan 32
Fettuccine with Artichokes and Roasted
    Peppers 33
Bacon and Parmesan Frittata 34
Fresh Tomato and Spinach Pasta
    Salad 36
Crab and Caper Bowtie Pasta 37
Creamy Macaroni and Cheese with
    Fresh Tomato Slices 39
Wild Mushroom and Parmesan
    Fettuccine 40
Spaghetti Carbonara with Bacon 41
Spaghetti with Red Clam Sauce 43
Quick Spaghetti with Tomato Basil
    Sauce 44

Pasta Shells with Aromatic Meatballs 45
Quick Pasta with Roasted Eggplant 46
Easy Tomato and Tuna Pasta 47
Pumpkin, Ricotta and Pesto Pasta 48
Tossed Oriental Noodles with Sweet
    Chili Dressing 50

Rice
Quick Seafood Paella 53
Simple Mushroom Risotto 54
Fried Rice with Bacon and Chinese
    Greens 56
Chicken Rice Pilaf 57

Chicken
Pan-fried Chicken with Mustard Sauce 58
Grilled Chicken with Aromatic Spice
    Rub 60
Stuffed Chicken Breasts Wrapped in
    Prosciutto 61
Creamy Chicken Kiev 62
Baked Chicken Fingers with Tartar
    Sauce 64
Simple Coq Au Vin 65
Fragrant Chicken Curry with Toasted
    Almonds 66
Chinese Stir-fry with Chicken and
    Cashews 68
Chicken with Honey Lemon Sauce 69
Cajun Chicken with Rémoulade
    Sauce 70

Meat
Perfect Steaks 72
Lamb Chops with Creamy White
    Beans 74
Grilled Lamb Chops with Pesto Sauce 75
Quick Beef Kebabs 76
Irish Lamb Stew 77
Moroccan Lamb with Couscous
    or Rice 78

Mongolian Lamb 80
Braised Pork Chops with Herbs 81
Pork Cutlets with Zesty Tomato Sauce 83
Beef Fajitas with Two Salsas 84
Beef and Tofu Sukiyaki 87

Seafood
Baked Fish with Fresh Tomatoes and
    Basil 88
Pan-fried Fish with Snow Peas and
    Almonds 90
Scallops on the Half Shell with Garlic
    Basil Butter 91
Simple Shrimp Risotto 92
Barbecued Shrimp with Toasted
    Polenta 93
Mussels Steamed in Wine 94
Crunchy Calamari Rings 95
Fish Steaks with Citrus and Basil
    Salsa 96
Oriental Fish with Cilantro Rice 98
Baked Mediterranean-Style Fish 99
Quick Fish and Chips 100
Pan-fried Fish with Lemon and
    Capers 102
Seared Tuna Steaks with Mexican
    Salsa 103

Desserts
Quick Banana and Raspberry
    Soufflé 104
Easy Lime and Blueberry Crème
    Brûlée 105
Cinnamon Crumbled Banana Cups 106
Poached Peaches with Sweet Ricotta
    Cream 108
Baked Stuffed Apples 109
Fruit Poached in Sweet Red Wine 110
Fresh Summer Fruit Salad 111

Fresh and Simple Cooking

We live in an age when every aspect of our lives has been sped up, and we all seem to have less time to do anything. There are many one-parent families and families where both parents go to work, and more young people whose careers are so competitive that their working hours seem to eat away at much of their leisure time. Time to sit around a table for a shared meal seems impossible, and regular mealtimes seem like distant memories.

Fresh & Simple will help you to eat well even if your time is limited. There are dishes that take a few minutes to prepare and a few minutes to cook and there are others that are ready quickly but have a slightly longer cooking time. During that time, however, I'm sure a moment to sit down and enjoy a glass of wine, to ease back from yet another frantic day, would be welcome!

You'll find dishes in this book that can be enjoyed by anyone from children and teenagers to busy adults and those who would rather not spend endless hours in the kitchen. Specific starters have not been included, although there are a few desserts. However, there is no reason why one of the salads, or indeed a soup, could not be used as a starter.

Though the food in this book is fast, that doesn't mean that it's not good for you. A meal prepared in a few minutes can be just as tasty and nutritious as one that takes a couple of hours in the kitchen, battling through the latest trendy gourmet recipe book. Don't feel guilty using canned products, such as tomatoes or tuna in water, as these, combined with fresh ingredients, can form the basis for some great dishes. A meal prepared from this book at home will be far better than buying a take-out meal or zapping a frozen packaged dish in the microwave.

To keep the recipes in this book simple and quick it is important to be prepared. Before making any of the recipes, read through them and make sure that you have the ingredients on hand, or that you will be able to pick them up during the day. It is also recommended that you keep a few key ingredients in your pantry, particularly canned or frozen foods such as tomatoes, tuna, a variety of beans and corn. Extra virgin olive oil and some sunflower oil or vegetable oil are essential; stocks, tomato paste, vinegars, Asian sauces (such as soy and oyster) are also basic necessities. Pasta, couscous and rice store well for absolutely ages and form the basis for many recipes in this book and indeed for much of modern-day cooking. Although fresh herbs are quite often featured in this book, a small quantity of dried mixed herbs, oregano and sweet basil will always be useful if the fresh varieties are hard to come by. Jars of olives, artichoke hearts, pesto and sundried tomatoes are also useful for things like pasta sauces. Finally, a reasonable selection of spices will always come in handy, especially chili or cayenne, cinnamon, turmeric, cumin and a good-quality curry powder.

If you can't get fresh produce, which should always be the first choice when buying fruit or vegetables, then commercially frozen vegetables are the next best choice. Frozen versions of hard-to-buy items such as bean shoots or other Asian varieties are sometimes the only way to go. The fresher the produce, the better it is for you, and therefore frozen vegetables, which are frozen immediately after harvesting, are going to be better for you than vegetables that have been lying around in your local corner store for a week or more!

There are dishes in this book that will suit any occasion, whether it is something for the kids, something for a cold winter's night, or a dish to impress friends. Some of the recipes can be made in advance and frozen. Other dishes can be stored in the refrigerator for a few days.

Considering the ease with which these recipes can be made, we hope that you try to eat at least one home-cooked meal a day—preferably served at the table. This way of eating is good for your digestion, so you'll get the maximum benefit from whatever you eat. It also enables you to enjoy and share the pleasure of eating and conversation with your family or friends.

Cooking Methods and Tips

The recipes in this book are based on the idea that a well-stocked pantry and a small supply of a few fresh, refrigerated items can provide the basis for impromptu, hassle-free meals. If your cupboards and refrigerator are stocked with these suggested ingredients, you'll find it very easy to whip a delicious, wholesome meal.

Herbs, spices and seasonings:
• fresh herbs—chives, parsley, basil, coriander leaves (cilantro) • dried herbs—oregano, thyme, sage, rosemary, dill, bay leaves • seasonings and spices—salt, black pepper, ground cinnamon, nutmeg, mixed spice, chili flakes or cayenne pepper, paprika, cumin, fennel or caraway seeds • exotic extras—Mexican-style chili powder, Chinese five-spice powder, garam masala, curry paste.

Stocks: • fish, chicken, beef or vegetable, canned or frozen, bouillon cubes or powder, canned consommé.

Sauces, condiments and dressings:
• savory sauces—Worcestershire, Tabasco, ketchup • Oriental extras—mirin or sake (substitute dry sherry), soy, hot or sweet chili, oyster • condiments—honey, fruit chutney, marmalade, redcurrant jelly, Dijon and English mustards, gherkin relish, mint sauce, tomato salsa • dressings—egg mayonnaise, vinegar (red or white wine, cider or malt), oil (vegetable or peanut, olive).

Canned and packaged goods:
• whole peeled tomatoes, tuna or salmon, condensed soups, coconut cream, tomato paste, evaporated milk, red kidney or cannellini beans, pineapple pieces • delicatessen delicacies—anchovy fillets, capers, marinated artichoke hearts or olives, sun-dried tomatoes.

Fresh and frozen produce: for flavoring—onions, garlic, ginger, lemons • for salads—celery, green or red bell pepper, green onions (scallions), red onion, cucumber, assorted salad leaves • everyday standbys—tomatoes, potatoes, carrots, frozen green peas, frozen spinach.

Refrigerated items: • milk, cream, butter and/or margarine, eggs, cheese (including parmesan, cheddar), plain yogurt or sour cream, bacon.

Basic staples: • flour—all-purpose (plain), self-raising • sugar—granulated, confectioner's (icing); brown (light and dark) • baking basics—leavening (baking powder, bicarbonate of soda/baking soda), cocoa powder or cooking chocolate, unsweetened shredded (desiccated) coconut, vanilla extract (essence) • dried fruit—apricots, golden raisins (sultanas), dates • thickeners—cornstarch or arrowroot • coatings—dry breadcrumbs, soda crackers (saltines) • cereals—bread, rice (white, brown), pasta (including elbow macaroni, spaghetti), polenta, cracked wheat (burghul), couscous • nuts and seeds—pine nuts, walnuts, blanched slivered almonds, sesame seeds.

To cook perfect pasta:
1 Add lots of water and a generous amount of salt to a tall pot. Bring to a rapid boil.
2 Add all the pasta, stir to ensure none of it is sticking together, and continue to stir throughout cooking.
3 Do not overcook. Check the pasta a few minutes before you think it will be done and keep checking until it is al dente (meaning it offers only just a little resistance when bitten).
4 Drain in a colander and serve immediately. Cooking time depends on the shape and size of the pasta. If you can't serve it straight away, toss with a little olive oil to keep moist. You should do this if you are storing leftover pasta too. If you need to keep the pasta warm, return it to the dry but warm pan and cover. To reheat already-cooked pasta, add it to boiling water for about 30 seconds. Fresh pasta keeps for a few days in the refrigerator. Dried pasta keeps almost indefinitely.

Great rice: There is a variety of white rice available, including long-grain, short-grain, and arborio rice, and perfumed long-grain rices such as basmati and jasmine. There is also wild rice. Which is not a rice at all, but a kind of aquatic sea grass. Store white rice in a sealed container in a cool, dark place; it will keep for over a year. Brown rice will keep for a few months if stored in the refrigerator. Most rice can be cooked using the absorption method. For each cup of rice, use the indicated amount of water: medium to long-grain rice—$1^3/_4$ –2 cups, short-grain rice—$1^1/_2$–2 cups, basmati—$1^1/_2$ cups. First, rinse rice well. Place in a saucepan with water and bring mixture to a boil over high heat. Stir once, cover tightly, and reduce heat to low. Cook according to the time indicated on the packet, usually 15 to 20 minutes, without lifting lid. If all water has not been absorbed, cover again and cook for a few more minutes. When done, fluff rice with a fork and let stand, covered for a few minutes off the heat. Cook rice in stock or add herbs to the cooking water for flavor.

Classic mashed potatoes: Peel and cut large baking potatoes in quarters and place in cold salted water to cover. Bring to a boil and cook covered until tender, about 20–30 minutes. Test with a skewer. Drain, then return to hot saucepan and leave for a couple of minutes until extra moisture evaporates, shaking occasionally. Add hot milk, butter, salt, and pepper and mash with a fork until smooth. If you like your potatoes extra creamy, beat with a wooden spoon. Try adding a finely chopped white onion or green onion and a chopped garlic clove while mashing. Or add grated gruyere or cheddar cheese.

Dried beans: Pulses is the general name for dried beans, peas, and lentils. They make a great basis for a meal as they are inexpensive, simple to prepare, very filling, and high in protein.

Some of the most popular are:
• haricot or white beans—these include navy beans, soissons and flageolets • cannellini beans • butter or lima beans • borlotti beans • chick peas, ceci peas, or garbanzo beans • red kidney beans • broad or fava beans • blackeyed beans or peas. You can store dried pulses, tightly sealed, in a dark, dry place for up to a year. You can also buy most pulses already prepared and canned, which reduces time and effort. To cook dry beans, rinse thoroughly first and sort out any undesirable pieces. Cover with water and soak for several hours or overnight. Rinse, then cover with fresh water in a saucepan and simmer until tender. You can add garlic, bay leaves, chili, or other spices but don't add salt, sugar, or acids (such as tomatoes) until after cooking, as this can toughen the beans. Dried lentils need no presoaking, and small red lentils only take about 15 minutes to cook. Brown and green lentils take a little longer. Place in a saucepan with enough cold water to cover. Bring to a boil then simmer until just tender, not mushy.

Equipment for Simple Cooking
Hand tools: • knives—paring (long and short-bladed, one serrated), cleaver (chopper), carver • graduated measuring spoons and cups, 2-cup measuring cup with a pouring spout, slotted spoon, tongs, wooden spoons, egg flip (pancake turner), whisk, meat fork, ladle, kitchen shears, flexible-bladed metal spatulas (long and short), rubber spatula (scraper), flat fish server, can opener, potato masher, vegetable peeler, apple corer.

Utensils: • mixing—glass or metal bowls of graduated sizes • baking—oven gloves or cloth, sifter or sieve, baking sheets, pie pan (flan ring) with removable base, fluted quiche dish, pie dishes (1 fruit plate, 1 oval dish for meat), springform or round cake pans, square pan, muffin pan, loaf pan, wire cooling rack • roasting—roasting pan, roasting rack, baking dish with lid, meat thermometer • stove-top cooking—saucepans with lids: small (with pouring spout), medium and large, double boiler insert (or heatproof bowl to fit pan); frying pans (large and small, nonstick), crepe/omelet pan, wok, flameproof casserole dish or Dutch oven with lid (preferably cast iron).

Accessories: • paper towels, foil, greaseproof (waxed) paper, baking (parchment) paper, plastic food wrap and bags • 2–3 cutting boards • citrus juicer • screw-top jar for dressings, salad bowl and serving tongs • sieve (1 small, 1 large), colander • metal steamer insert or bamboo or metal steamer • grater (shredder) • bamboo and metal skewers, toothpicks, kitchen string • brushes for pastry and basting • heatproof bowls (ramekins).

Appliances: • hand-held electric mixer, small blender, standard food processor.

Essential Ingredients

Bok choy is an Asian green vegetable with thick white stems and mild-flavored dark green leaves. Baby bok choy and Shanghai bok choy are also available. Can be substituted in recipes by Chinese broccoli, choy sum, or other leafy greens.

Capers are the small buds of a Mediterranean bush, generally pickled in brine and used whole as a flavoring or garnish. They are sold in jars in the condiments section of supermarkets. Store opened jars in the refrigerator. Capers are also available preserved in salt, which should be rinsed off before using.

Coriander leaves are also known as cilantro or Chinese parsley. Available fresh, the leaves are strongly flavored, so use sparingly.

Cardamom is an Indian spice that comes in the form of large green or brown pods containing seeds with a string lemony flavor. It is available ground but for best flavor, grind your own just before using.

Cumin seeds are available whole or ground, and have a powerful earthy, nutty flavor and aroma.

Fish sauce is a very pungent, strong-flavored and salty sauce extracted from fermented fish. Flavor and saltiness differ with different brands. Fish sauce from Thailand, called *nam pla*, is commonly available. Don't be put off by the strong fishy smell as this disappears once the sauce is cooked. There is really no substitute.

Pine nuts are the small ivory-colored seeds of pine trees. When raw, the seeds have a soft texture and a sweet, buttery flavor. They are often lightly toasted to bring out their flavor and to add a crunchy texture. Pine nuts can be found in most supermarkets.

Polenta refers to a specially ground cornmeal and to the dish into which it is made. The cornmeal is cooked and often enriched with butter, cream, cheese, or eggs. Cold polenta can be shaped and grilled.

Saffron is known as the queen of spices and is very expensive. You may substitute ground turmeric though it has neither the subtlety nor the strength.

Thyme is a fragrant herb. It has a faint lemony flavor and powerful antiseptic and preservative qualities. Because fresh thyme has a mild flavor, it is difficult to overpower a dish. Use the small, tender leaves and discard the woody stems. Use fresh thyme rather than dried thyme whenever possible.

Yellow bean sauce is a richly-flavored seasoning made from fermented soybeans, similar to Japanese miso (which may be used as a substitute) and is available in jars. They vary in color from dark brown to light golden.

Simple Potato and Leek Soup

Potatoes and leeks are a classic vegetable soup combination that always satisfies. When served chilled, this soup is known by the elegant name *vichyssoise*; when served hot, well, it's just plain ole potato and leek soup. Ground coriander seeds give our version a special twist and delightful aroma.

3 tablespoons butter
3 large leeks, trimmed of most green and finely sliced
1 onion, peeled and thinly sliced
1 lb (500 g) potatoes, peeled and diced
4 cups (900 ml) chicken or vegetable stock
Salt and ground white pepper, to taste
$1/4$ teaspoon ground coriander
1 egg yolk
$2/3$ cup (150 ml) light cream
Snipped chives, to serve

Serves 6

1 Melt the butter in a large saucepan and stir-fry the leek and onion very gently for about 5 minutes, without browning. Add the potato, stock and seasonings and ground coriander and bring to a boil. Cover and simmer gently for about 30 minutes, or until the vegetables are very tender.
2 Cool a little, then sieve or blend the soup in a blender or food processor and pour into a clean saucepan.
3 Blend the egg yolk with the cream and whisk evenly into the soup. Reheat gently without boiling, adjust the seasonings, cool, then chill thoroughly.
4 Serve sprinkled liberally with the snipped chives.

Note: This classic dish may also be served hot—simply serve after reheating.

New England Clam Chowder

Creamy and rich, this easy-to-make chowder is perfect for a cold winter's evening.

2 strips bacon, diced
1 small onion, diced
3 large potatoes, peeled and diced to yield
  3 cups
Salt and ground white pepper, to taste
14-oz (400-g) can clams, drained and
  chopped, reserving the liquid
1¹/₂ cups (375 ml) fish stock or water
¹/₂ cup (125 ml) light cream
¹/₂ cup (125 ml) milk

Serves 2–4

1 Fry the bacon in a saucepan over low heat until crisp. Add the onion and stir-fry over medium heat until soft. Add the potatoes and toss through. Add the salt and pepper, reserved 1¹/₂ cups (375ml) clam liquid and stock. Simmer for 15 minutes, until the potatoes are tender.
2 Add the clams, cream and milk, and gently heat through. Let stand if possible (see below). Reheat if necessary and serve warm.

Note: Chowder improves over time, so let it stand off the heat for 1 hour or refrigerate overnight before reheating. Serve topped with fresh chopped chives or thyme and freshly ground black pepper. Salted crackers are the traditional accompaniment.

Chunky Vegetable Soup

For the best results, make this nourishing and delicious vegetable soup with in-season produce.

6 small new potatoes
2¹/₂ lbs (1.25 kg) assorted vegetables (young turnips, carrots, zucchini, summer squash)
2 large onions, peeled and chopped
2 cloves garlic, peeled and chopped
1 stick celery, trimmed and chopped
1 tablespoon oil
3 cups (750 ml) tomato juice
3 cups (750 ml) chicken or vegetable stock
2–3 sprigs fresh parsley, chopped
2 tablespoon chopped fresh basil
Freshly ground black pepper, to taste
Crusty bread, to serve

1 Cut the potatoes and vegetables into 1-in (2.5-cm) chunks. Add the potatoes and harder vegetables to the pan. Reduce the heat and simmer for 12 to 15 minutes, or until the vegetables are almost tender.
2 Heat the oil in a large, heavy-based saucepan over medium heat and cook the onion, garlic and celery stirring, for 5 minutes or until golden. Add the juice and stock to the pan and bring to a boil.
3 Add the other vegetables to the pan with the parsley, basil and pepper to taste. Simmer, stirring occasionally, for 10 minutes or until the vegetables are tender. Serve in heated deep soup plates with the crusty bread.

Serves 4–6

Hearty Fish Stew

This healthy meal-in-one stew is packed with flavor, and yet has very little fat—making it a great weekly mainstay. A touch of hot pepper sauce adds some pizzazz to this simple meal—to ratchet up the weekday dinner heat, just add a few drops more.

1 small leek
1 onion
2 cloves garlic
2 tablespoons oil
14-oz (400-g) can whole, peeled tomatoes
3 cups (750 ml) fish stock or water
2 tablespoons each chopped fresh basil
   and parsley
1 tablespoon chopped fresh thyme
1 bay leaf
2–3 drops hot pepper sauce, such as Tabasco
2 lbs (1 kg) boneless white-fleshed fish
   fillets (e.g. bream, snapper, ling, cod)
Freshly ground black pepper, to taste
Parsley sprigs, to serve

Serves 6

1 Remove the green part of the leek, halve the white part lengthwise. Wash clean under cold running water, drain and slice thinly crosswise. Peel and thinly slice the onion. Peel and finely chop the garlic.
2 Heat the oil in a large, heavy-based saucepan. Cook the leek, onion and garlic over medium heat, stirring, for 5 minutes, or until golden.
3 Crush the tomatoes and add with their juice to the pan. Add the stock, herbs and hot pepper sauce. Bring to a boil, reduce the heat and simmer for 25 to 30 minutes.
4 Cut the fish into large, bite-size pieces, add to the pan and simmer for 5 to 10 minutes, or until tender. Season to taste with the black pepper.
5 Ladle the fish and stock into wide, deep soup plates. Serve garnished with parsley.

Notes:
1. Any combination of firm white-fleshed (non-oily) fish can be used to make a simple soup-stew.
2. Serve with a good white wine and crusty bread.
3. For the look and taste of the French fish soup known as bouillabaisse, replace $3/4$ cup (180 ml) of the stock or water in this recipe with dry white wine and add 2 to 3 thin strips of orange rind (scraping off all the white pith) and a pinch of saffron powder or ground turmeric when you add the stock.

Bean and Pasta Soup

Italians call it *pasta e fagioli*. In our delicious version we use lima beans and black-eyed peas and add some bacon—the great flavor enhancer. For quickest results, use canned bean.

1 onion, diced
3 sticks celery, sliced
4 slices smoked streaky bacon, chopped
1 tablespoon oil
5 cups (1.25 liters) beef stock
1 cup (175 g) cooked or canned black-eyed
   peas
1 cup (175 g) cooked or canned lima beans
1 lb (500 g) Pipe rigate, conchigilie, penne,
   or rigatoni pasta
Salt and freshly ground black pepper,
   to taste

1 Fry the onion, celery and bacon in the oil in a large pan for 2 to 3 minutes. Add the stock and beans, bring to a boil, cover the pan and simmer for 30 minutes.
2 Add the pasta to the pan and cook for a further 10 to 15 minutes, until the pasta is tender. Season to taste.

Note: Try using other beans, such as cannellini, borlotti or red kidney beans, or a combination of three or four.

Serves 4–6

Red Cabbage and Beef Borscht

Beets give borscht its signature red hue. This version, with beef and cabbage, is a great meal-in-one soup.

1 lb (500 g) lean beef
1 onion, diced
1–2 tablespoons oil
1 lb (500 g) fresh beets, peeled and grated
4 cups (350 g) thinly sliced red cabbage
5 cups (1.25 liters) beef stock
2 tablespoons red wine vinegar
1 tablespoon tomato ketchup
Salt and freshly ground black pepper, to taste
1 teaspoon dried thyme
1 large or 2 small potatoes, peeled and diced
$^1/_2$ cup (125 ml) sour cream
1 teaspoon fennel seeds, to garnish
2 teaspoons chopped fresh dill, to garnish

1 Slice the beef into small pieces.
2 Cook the onion and beef in the oil in a large covered pan until the beef is brown. Add the beets, cabbage, stock, vinegar, tomato ketchup, salt, pepper and thyme. Bring to a boil, reduce the heat and simmer for 40 minutes.
3 Add the potatoes to the pan and cook for a further 10 minutes. Divide the soup among six warmed bowls. Put 1 tablespoon of the sour cream into the middle of each bowl, then sprinkle with fennel seeds and dill.

Serves 4–6

Chinese Chicken Noodle Soup

This Chinese version of a classic soup will give comfort on a cold day and delight the palate.

12 cups (2.75 liters) chicken stock
8 oz (250 g) dried Chinese egg noodles
4–8 tablespoons soy sauce
4 tablespoons oyster sauce
Salt, to taste
2–4 tablespoons dry sherry, (optional)
Fresh red chili pepper, to taste (either chopped or as a sauce or paste from a jar)
4 cups (750 g) cooked leftover shredded chicken meat

Serves 4

1 Heat the stock in a saucepan. Boil the dried noodles in the stock for a few minutes or according to packet directions. Add the soy and oyster sauces, salt and sherry. Taste and adjust seasonings as required. Add the chili.
2 Place the chicken in four soup bowls. Pour the stock and noodles over the chicken and serve hot.

Notes:
1. Chopped ham may be used in place of chicken, use $1/4$ cup (30 g) chopped ham.
2. For variation use rice noodles instead of egg noodles.
3. For a healthy version, add cabbage, bok choy or steamed broccoli and garnish with chopped green onions (scallions).

French Onion Soup

Served with a simple green salad, this rich soup makes a light yet satisfying meal.

3 tablespoons butter
1 lb (500 g) onions, thinly sliced
1 cup (250 ml) dry white wine
$^1/_2$ cup (125 ml) water
5 cups (1.25 liters) beef or chicken stock
Salt and freshly ground black pepper,
  to taste
Baguettes (French bread), sliced and
  toasted, to serve
Gruyère cheese, freshly grated, to serve

Serves 4–6

1 Melt the butter in a deep, heavy-bottomed pan. Add the onions, wine and water and cook very gently on low heat until the onions are soft, about 30 to 40 minutes, stirring regularly. Add the stock and season to taste. Bring to a boil, cover and simmer for 10 minutes.
2 Meanwhile, top the toasted bread with the grated cheese and broil (grill) until the cheese is melted and golden.
3 Divide the soup among individual bowls and top each with a slice or two of the toasted bread. Serve immediately.

Note: You can also place unmelted cheese and toast on top of the individual soup bowls and then pop the whole lot under the broiler (grill) so that the entire top is covered with cheese.

Classic Potato Salad

This creamy potato salad, brightened with fresh parsley and crunchy celery, goes great with sandwiches or grilled meats.

2 lbs (1 kg) new potatoes
Fresh Vinaigrette Salad Dressing (see below)
2 sticks celery, trimmed and sliced
4 green onions (scallions), trimmed and sliced
1 cup (250 ml) mayonnaise
$1/2$ cup (125 ml) sour cream
$1^1/_2$ teaspoons Dijon mustard or horseradish cream
Freshly ground black pepper, to taste
Fresh parsley, chopped, to garnish

Serves 6–8

1 Place the potatoes in a saucepan with enough lightly salted water to cover. Bring to a boil and cook for 10 to 12 minutes, or until just tender. Drain and cool until easy to handle. Peel, if desired, and cut into thick pieces.
2 Place the warm potatoes in a bowl, drizzle with the Fresh Vinaigrette Salad Dressing and toss lightly to coat. Cover and refrigerate for 1 to 2 hours, or until cold.
3 Add the celery and green onions to the potatoes.
4 Combine the mayonnaise, sour cream and mustard in a bowl. Season to taste with the black pepper. Lightly fold the mixture through the potatoes. Refrigerate until required. Serve well chilled, sprinkled with parsley.

Note: Choose waxy, red-skinned potato that keeps its shape when cooked. Avoid overcooking—potatoes should be just tender when pierced with a skewer. Omit garlic from the Vinaigrette Dressing for milder flavor. Add fresh dill or chives instead. Add 1 to 2 chopped or sliced hard-boiled eggs, if desired. Make the salad ahead and refrigerate, covered, overnight to let the flavors mingle.

Fresh Vinaigrette Salad Dressing

With this tried-and-true salad dressing on hand, you can have a fresh green salad on the table in minutes.

1 clove garlic
1 teaspoon Dijon mustard
Pinch of sugar
Freshly ground black pepper, to taste
1 tablespoon white or red wine vinegar or
   lemon juice
4–5 tablespoons virgin olive oil

Peel and halve the garlic. Place all the ingredients in a screw-top jar. Cover and shake until blended. Or, whisk together the first 5 ingredients in a small bowl. Gradually add the oil, whisking constantly, until the dressing thickens slightly. Stand the dressing at room temperature to develop the flavors, while preparing the salad ingredients. Remove the garlic and shake or whisk again before serving.

Oriental Chicken Salad

Crystallized ginger gives this lemony chicken salad a pleasant sweetness.

4 boneless chicken breasts
Salt and pepper, to taste
3 tablespoons butter
$1^1/_2$ tablespoons chopped crystallized (candied) ginger or 1 tablespoon peeled and chopped ginger plus $1^1/_2$ tablespoons sugar
Grated rind and juice of 1 lemon
3–4 tablespoons sherry
Shredded lettuce
Sliced green onions (scallions), to serve
Fried Bread Croutons (see note), to serve

Serves 4

1 Remove any skin from the chicken and cut the flesh into strips. Season with the salt and pepper.
2 Melt the butter in a pan and fry the chicken briskly until lightly browned and cooked almost through, about 10 minutes. Add the ginger, lemon rind and juice, and sherry. Bring slowly to a boil. Simmer gently for 3 to 4 minutes then adjust the seasonings.
3 Serve on a bed of shredded lettuce sprinkled with green onions and garnished with the fried bread croutons

Note: To make Fried Bread Croutons, cut slices of brown or white bread into small cubes. Fry in shallow oil for 2 to 3 minutes on each side until browned, then drain on paper towels.

Thai Grilled Beef Salad

Spicy yet minty cool, this popular Thai salad is a summertime favorite lunch or dinnertime meal.

$1^1/_2$ lbs (700 g) boneless sirloin
4 tablespoons lime juice
4 tablespoons fish sauce
2 finger-length red chili peppers, deseeded
  and finely chopped
1 clove garlic, finely chopped
1 tablespoon grated fresh ginger
1 teaspoon shaved palm sugar
$^1/_2$ head lettuce
1 large onion
1 small hothouse (English) cucumber
2 tablespoons chopped basil or mint leaves
2 tablespoons chopped coriander leaves
  (cilantro)

1 Sear the steak in a hot frying pan for a few minutes each side, until cooked; try to leave it pink in the middle. Remove the meat from the heat and let it rest by placing it on a cool surface.
2 Combine the lime juice, fish sauce, chilies, garlic, ginger and sugar and set aside.
3 Tear the lettuce into pieces, cut the onion into thin wedges, slice the cucumber into thin strips. Arrange in a large bowl.
4 Add the basil and coriander leaves to the dressing and pour over the salad.
5 Slice the meat into very thin strips. Add to the salad, toss and serve.

Serves 2–4

Vegetarian Pasta Salad with Olives

To make your pasta salad really shine, always use the freshest vegetables and herbs possible.

8 oz (250 g) small pasta shells
Double quantity Fresh Vinaigrette Salad
    Dressing (page 20)
1 red onion, peeled and thinly sliced
2–3 sticks celery, trimmed and thinly sliced
4–6 radishes, trimmed and thinly sliced
8 black olives, pitted and halved
10 cherry tomatoes, halved
4 tablespoons chopped fresh parsley
Lettuce leaves, to serve

Serves 1–2 hours

1 Cook the pasta in a large saucepan of lightly salted boiling water until al dente. Drain well. Rinse under cold running water and drain again.
2 Transfer to a salad bowl. Prepare the Fresh Vinaigrette Salad Dressing according to the recipe on page 20 and combine with the pasta. Add the vegetables and chopped parsley to the bowl. Toss lightly, cover and refrigerate for 1 to 2 hours.
3 To serve, arrange the lettuce in a shallow serving plate or bowl and spoon the salad over.

Note: For a main course salad, add any of the following before serving: sliced of cooked ham or chicken, drained can of tuna in brine, sliced hard-boiled eggs, or toasted pine nuts, walnuts or pecans.

Warm Main-course Spinach Salad

This delicious and hearty salad is tossed with a warmed vinegar mixture that's sweet and spicy.

12 oz (350 g) young spinach leaves
$1/3$ cup (80 ml) oil
$1/2$ cup (60 g) coarsely chopped walnuts
4 slices prosciutto ham or bacon
1 clove garlic, peeled and chopped
2–3 tablespoon red wine vinegar or lemon juice
1 teaspoon sugar
$1/4$ teaspoon dried chili flakes (optional)
$1/4$ cup (60 g) crumbled goat or feta cheese, to serve

Serves 4

1 Rinse the spinach under cold running water, drain and dry with paper towels. Remove the tough stems and tear larger leaves into smaller pieces then place in a serving bowl.
2 Heat the oil in a frying pan over medium heat. Add the walnuts and cook, stirring, for 1 minute, or until golden. Remove from the heat. Remove the nuts immediately with a slotted spoon and scatter over the spinach.
3 Cut the prosciutto or bacon into thick strips. Return the pan to the heat and cook the prosciutto or bacon and the garlic, stirring, for 2 to 3 minutes, or until the prosciutto is crisp and golden.
4 Add the vinegar, sugar and chili flakes to the pan and simmer, stirring for 30 seconds. Spoon the dressing over the salad, toss lightly and sprinkle with the crumbled cheese. Serve immediately.

Mediterranean Pasta Salad

With the addition of savory and satisfying Canadian bacon, this elegant pasta salad is a quick meal-in-one.

8 plum tomatoes
2 cloves garlic, minced
3 tablespoons olive oil
2 tablespoons balsamic vinegar
$^1/_4$ cup (10 g) chopped fresh basil leaves
6 slices Canadian bacon
1 large red onion, sliced
1 cup (250 g) crumbled goat cheese or
  feta cheese
1 lb (500 g) pasta, cooked and drained

Serves 6

1 Heat the oven to 325°F (160°C). Cut the tomatoes in half and arrange on the baking sheet. Combine the garlic, 2 tablespoons oil, vinegar and $^1/_2$ of the basil leaves in a small bowl and mix well. Spoon a little of the oil mixture onto each tomato. Broil (grill) the tomatoes under low heat for 30 minutes.
2 Broil (grill) the Canadian bacon until crisp, about 1 minute on each side. Toss the onion in the remaining oil, arrange the slices on the baking sheet and broil (grill) under high heat for 2 minutes or until slightly softened and lightly browned.
3 Cut the goat cheese into $^1/_2$-in (12-mm) cubes. Toss the pasta with the cheese, onion and remaining basil leaves. Top with the tomatoes and Canadian bacon. Serve warm or cool.

Thai Chicken Noodle Salad

Coconut milk, a classic Thai ingredient, gives this aromatic noodle salad an extra rich flavor.

$1/2$ cup (125 ml) canned coconut milk
2 teaspoons fish sauce
2 teaspoons shaved palm sugar
2 teaspoons rice vinegar or white vinegar
1 teaspoon grated fresh ginger
1 red finger-length chili pepper, chopped finely
1 clove garlic, minced
12 oz (350 g) dried egg noodles
$1^1/4$ cups (90 g) snow peas
10 oz (300 g) boneless chicken thigh fillets
3 green onions (scallions), cut into strips
$1/2$ cup (30 g) coriander leaves (cilantro)
1 cucumber, sliced
$1/2$ red bell pepper, deseeded and thinly sliced

1 Whisk together the coconut milk, fish sauce, sugar, vinegar, ginger, chili and garlic. Set aside.
2 Cook the noodles according to package instructions. Drain and set aside. Blanch and slice the snow peas.
3 Meanwhile, grill or broil the chicken for 4 to 5 minutes each side, until cooked through. Let cool slightly. Slice and combine with the cooked noodles and the remaining ingredients while still warm. Stir through the coconut mixture dressing and serve immediately.

Serves 2

Fresh Potato Curry with Peas

Five different spices give this simple curried vegetable dish—made with just potatoes and peas—its enticing aroma and flavor. Served with rice and a green salad, Fresh Potato Curry with Peas is a satisfying vegetarian meal. It also pairs well with Fragrant Chicken Curry with Toasted Almonds (page 66).

$1^1/_2$ lbs (700 g) potatoes
2 tablespoons oil
2 cloves garlic, minced
1 medium onion, diced
2 teaspoon grated fresh ginger
2 teaspoons bottled chili paste (see note) or minced fresh red finger-length chili peppers
$^1/_4$ teaspoon cardamom seeds, cracked
$^1/_2$ teaspoon cumin seeds
1 teaspoon ground turmeric
$^1/_2$ teaspoon garam masala (see note)
1 teaspoon salt
Pepper, to taste
$^1/_4$ teaspoon ground cinnamon
3 cloves
1 bay leaf
1 tablespoon lemon juice
1 cup (150g) fresh or frozen peas

Serves 4

1 Peel and cut the potatoes into large chunks. Parboil the potatoes in salted water for 10 minutes. Drain and set aside.
2 Heat the oil in a large saucepan. Add the garlic and onion and stir-fry until the onion is soft. Add the spices and lemon juice and fry gently for a few minutes.
3 Add the potatoes, peas and water to the onion mixture and mix well to combine. Cover tightly and cook 10 minutes. Serve hot with cooked white rice.

Notes:
Garam masala is an Indian blend of powdered spices, usually including salt, cinnamon, cardamom, cloves, fennel and black pepper. Pre-blended garam masala can be bought from any store specializing in spices. Store in an airtight jar away from heat or sunlight. A bit of curry powder or ground fennel and cardamom mixed with salt may be used as a substitute.

Chili paste consists of ground fresh chilies, sometimes mixed with other ingredients such as vinegar, garlic or black beans, and commonly sold in jars. You may make your own and store it in the refrigerator, or purchase ready-made chili paste in Asian markets and well-stocked supermarkets.

Spinach and Cheese Frittata

In this easy-to-make Italian version of an omelet, all the ingredients are mixed together and then baked.

2 teaspoons oil
4 green onions (scallions), chopped
2 slices bacon, chopped
1 clove garlic, minced
2 cups (270 g) cooked, drained spinach
$1/2$ cup (30 g) chopped fresh basil
$1/2$ cup (150 g) fresh ricotta cheese
$1/3$ cup (90 g) crumbled feta cheese
2 tablespoons freshly grated Parmesan
2 eggs
1 cup (250 ml) milk
Salt and freshly ground pepper, to taste

1 Heat the oil in a frying pan over medium heat. Add the green onions, bacon and garlic and cook for 5 minutes.
2 Heat the oven to 350°F (180°C) if you will be baking the tart (it can also be microwaved).
3 Transfer the bacon mixture to a bowl and stir in the spinach, basil and cheeses. Place in a microwave-proof or ovenproof pie dish. Combine the eggs and milk and pour over. Season with salt and pepper.
4 Bake for 30 minutes or microwave on high until set, 10 to 15 minutes.
5 Serve warm, cut into wedges.

Serves 2–3

Beef Stroganoff with Egg Noodles

This famous dish is surprisingly quick to make. Rich and creamy, it's a great choice for a winter's day.

1 tablespoon oil
$1/_2$ small onion, sliced
1 cup (90 g) sliced button mushrooms
10 oz (300 g) beef fillet, cut into thin slices
$1/_4$ teaspoon ground red pepper (cayenne)
Salt and freshly ground pepper, to taste
$1/_2$ cup (125 ml) sour cream
$1/_2$ cup (125 ml) beef stock
8 oz (250 g) dried egg noodles 1 lb (500 g)
  fresh noodles, cooked, drained and buttered
1 tablespoon chopped fresh parsley, to garnish

Serves 3–4

1 Heat 2 teaspoons of the oil in a frying pan over medium heat. Add the onion and mushrooms and cook, partially covered, 3 to 4 minutes. Set aside.
2 Heat the remaining oil over high heat and cook the beef for 1 to 2 minutes, stirring. Season with ground red pepper (cayenne), salt and pepper.
3 Add the mushroom mixture, sour cream and stock to the beef and place over low heat until heated through, 1 to 2 minutes.
4 Serve the stroganoff over the noodles, sprinkled with parsley.

Note: Beef fillet is the best cut, as it does not need much cooking to become tender. If stock is unavailable, you can use water but the flavor won't be quite so good.

Fettuccine with Ham and Parmesan

A simplified and light Alfredo sauce envelopes fettuccine noodles, ham and Parmesan to create a tempting dish.

8 oz (250 g) dried fettuccine
$^1/_4$ cup (60 ml) white wine
$^2/_3$ cup (150 ml) light cream
$^1/_4$ cup (15 g) assorted chopped fresh
  herbs, such as rosemary, thyme, chives,
  parsley, basil and mint leaves
3–4 slices (4 oz/100 g) ham, thinly sliced
  into long strips
2 tablespoons freshly grated Parmesan
Salt and freshly ground pepper, to taste

Serves 2

1 Cook the pasta in a large saucepan of boiling salted water until al dente. Drain well.
2 While the pasta is cooking, place the wine in a saucepan and bring to a boil. Boil until the liquid is reduced by half (2 to 3 minutes). Stir in the cream and return to a boil. Reduce the heat and simmer. Add the herbs and ham and heat through for 1 minute.
3 Pour the sauce over the hot pasta and sprinkle with the Parmesan. Season with salt and pepper to taste.

Fettuccine with Artichokes and Roasted Peppers

This bright and colorful pasta dish is virtually fat free, making it an extremely quick and healthy supper.

3 large red bell peppers, halved and deseeded
4 tablespoons oil
1 clove garlic, finely chopped
12-oz (350-g) jar marinated artichoke
  hearts, with marinade
$1/_2$ cup (125 g) canned sardines, torn into
  pieces, or canned tuna (optional)
1 lb (500 g) dried fettuccine
Black pepper, cracked, to serve
Parmesan shavings, to serve (optional)

Serves 4

1 Place the bell peppers on a tray under a hot broiler (grill), skin side up and cook under high heat until the skin blackens and bubbles. Let cool slightly, peel off the skin and cut the bell peppers into strips.
2 Place the oil and garlic in a pan and cook over medium heat until the garlic is fragrant, about 1 minute.
3 Halve the artichoke hearts and add to the pan with 6 tablespoons of the artichoke marinade and red pepper strips. Stir-fry gently over very low heat while cooking the pasta. Add the sardines or tuna (if using) and heat through.
4 Cook the pasta until al dente, usually 5 to 12 minutes. Toss with the artichoke, peppers, sardines or tuna (if using) and oil. Serve with cracked pepper and Parmesan shavings.

Bacon and Parmesan Frittata

Sort of an Italian Mac 'n Cheese, this noodle-based frittata is a great way to use up leftover pasta. Virtually any type of pasta can be used, and any type of vegetable added. We enjoy this dish for supper and also for brunch.

1 tablespoon butter
2 tablespoons oil
2 cloves garlic, chopped
1 leek, chopped
2–3 strips bacon, chopped
4 eggs, lightly beaten
2 tablespoons milk or cream
Salt and freshly ground black pepper, to taste
1/2 cup (60 g) freshly grated Parmesan
8 oz (250 g) dried fettuccine or 1 lb (500 g) fresh, broken in half and cooked until al dente and drained

Serves 4

1 Melt the butter with 1 tablespoon of oil in a heavy-based frying pan. Add the garlic, leek and bacon and cook until the leek is soft, about 5 minutes. Remove from the pan; set aside.
2 Combine the eggs, milk, salt, lots of pepper and half the Parmesan in a large bowl. Mix in the cooked pasta.
3 Heat the remaining oil over low heat in the original pan. Add half the pasta mixture. Top with the bacon mixture, then the rest of the pasta mixture. Using a plate, press down firmly to pack tight. Sprinkle the remaining Parmesan on top.
4 Cook for 12 minutes to brown the bottom, then place under a hot broiler (grill) to set and brown the top.

Notes:
1. Serve frittata with bread and a green salad.
2. Try incorporating any chopped vegetables you have on hand— fresh tomato, mushrooms, bell peppers, broccoli or zucchini— instead of, or with, the leek at the start.
3. Substitute ham, salami, Canadian bacon, or leftover chicken or turkey for the bacon.
4. Herbs make a welcome addition, fresh or dried. Try basil, oregano, or thyme.
5. Add a handful of shredded mozzarella with the Parmesan if you like a cheesier taste. This will also help it to hold together.

Fresh Tomato and Spinach Pasta Salad

This delicious pasta dish couldn't be simpler. For best results, use garden-ripe tomatoes.

8 ripe tomatoes, halved
2 teaspoons chopped fresh basil or oregano
2 cloves garlic, chopped
4 strips bacon, chopped
4 tablespoons oil
Salt and freshly ground black pepper, to taste
1 bunch baby spinach, rinsed, thick stalks
   removed
1 lb (500 g) dried penne, cooked until al
   dente and drained
1/2 cup (60 g) pitted black olives
1/2 cup (120 g) freshly grated Parmesan

1 Preheat the oven to 400°F (200°C). Place the tomatoes (cut side up) in a baking dish. Scatter with the basil, garlic and bacon. Drizzle with the oil. Season with salt and pepper. Bake for 50–60 minutes, until very soft.
2 Place the drained pasta in a large bowl. Break up the tomatoes roughly and add, along with the pan juices, to the pasta. Add the spinach and olives and toss. Serve with the grated Parmesan on the side.

Serves 4

Crab and Caper Bowtie Pasta

This subtle yet rich pasta dish makes a complete meal when served with a simple green salad.

8 oz (250 g) bowtie pasta, cooked until
  al dente and drained
1 tablespoon white wine vinegar
2 green onions (scallions), chopped
$1/_2$ cup (125 ml) light cream
1 cup (180 g) cooked crabmeat
Grated rind of 1 small lime
2 tablespoons chopped fresh Italian parsley
  or coriander leaves (cilantro)
2 teaspoons drained capers
Salt and freshly ground pepper, to taste
Chopped fresh Italian parsley or coriander
  leaves (cilantro), to garnish

1 Combine the vinegar and green onions in a saucepan and bring to a boil. Simmer for 1 minute. Add all the remaining ingredients except the pasta and garnish and simmer for 2 minutes, or until heated through. Adjust the seasonings to taste.
2 Pour the crab mixture over the hot pasta, sprinkling with the extra parsley or coriander leaves if desired.

Note: Instead of crabmeat, you can use a drained small can of tuna or an 8 oz (250 g) poached white fish fillet or shrimp. Use two forks to flake the flesh.

Serves 2

Creamy Macaroni and Cheese with Fresh Tomato Slices

Even the classics need to be revisited from time to time. In our version of this all-time favorite dish, we've added meaty slices of fresh tomatoes for color and surprise flavor. All those who enjoy a slice of tomato in their grilled cheese sandwich will appreciate this recipe for mac 'n cheese.

8 oz (250 g) elbow macaroni
$^1/_2$ cup (125 g) cream cheese, at room temperature
2 teaspoons Dijon or wholegrain mustard
1 cup (250 g) grated cheddar
2 tomatoes
2 slices white sandwich bread, crusts removed
2 tablespoons chopped fresh parsley
2 tablespoons melted butter

White Sauce
4 tablespoons butter
4 tablespoons all-purpose (plain) flour
2 cups (500 ml) warmed milk
Salt and ground white or black pepper, to taste

Serves 6

1 Preheat the oven to 375°F (190°C). Cook the macaroni in a large saucepan of boiling, lightly salted water for 8 to 10 minutes (until al dente). Drain and return to the pan.
2 Make the White Sauce by melting the butter in a saucepan over medium heat. Add the flour. Using a whisk or wooden spoon, cook, stirring for 1 minute. Remove the pan from the heat. Gradually blend in the warmed milk. Return the pan to the heat and cook, stirring constantly, until the Sauce bubbles and thickens. Season to taste with salt and ground pepper.
3 Stir pieces of the cream cheese and mustard into the Sauce. Cook over medium heat, stirring, until the Sauce is smooth and thick. Remove the pan from the heat. Add the cheddar and stir until melted.
4 Pour the Sauce over the macaroni and mix well. Spread the mixture evenly in an 8-cup (2-liter) shallow ovenproof dish. Cut each tomato into 3 or 4 slices and arrange over the macaroni.
5 Finely crumble the bread with your fingers. Combine with the parsley and butter and sprinkle over the tomatoes.
6 Bake for 20 to 25 minutes, or until the mixture is bubbling and the top is golden.

Wild Mushroom and Parmesan Fettuccine

For best results, try a mixture of different types of mushrooms in this exotic pasta dish.

2 tablespoons oil
1 medium onion, finely chopped
3 cloves garlic, minced
3 cups (150 g) wild mushrooms or porcini
  mushrooms
1 lb (500 g) dried fettuccine, cooked until al
  dente and drained
$^3/_4$ cup (90 g) finely grated Parmesan
$1^1/_2$ cups (375 ml) half-and-half or light cream
3 tablespoons chopped fresh chives
Shaved Parmesan, to garnish

Serves 4

1 Heat the oil in a large frying pan over medium heat. Add the onion and garlic and cook, stirring, until the onion is soft. Add the mushrooms and cook, stirring, until just tender, about 3 minutes.
2 Add the grated Parmesan and cream to the mushrooms in the frying pan and cook, stirring occasionally, for 10 minutes or until the mixture has thickened slightly.
3 Stir in the chives and cooked fettuccine. Serve sprinkled with the shaved Parmesan.

Note: Any seasonal wild mushrooms can be used, but avoid using regular button mushrooms, as they don't have as much flavor.

Spaghetti Carbonara with Bacon

This protein-packed pasta dish is famous for its rich flavor. Our version has a touch of hot peppers.

1 lb (500 g) dried spaghetti, cooked until al dente and drained
5 tablespoons extra virgin olive oil
2 large cloves garlic, finely chopped
1–2 red finger-length chili peppers, deseeded and sliced (optional)
4 oz (125 g) bacon or Canadian bacon, chopped
2 eggs, lightly beaten
$1/2$ cup (60 g) freshly grated Parmesan
Freshly ground black pepper, to taste

Serves 4

1 Add the oil, garlic, chili and bacon to a large frying pan and cook over low heat for a few minutes, until the garlic is pale golden and the bacon has cooked.
2 Add the drained spaghetti to the frying pan. Take the pan off the heat and immediately add the eggs and Parmesan. Toss through, allowing the heat of the spaghetti to "cook" the eggs and Parmesan. Sprinkle the black pepper over the spaghetti and serve immediately.

Note: For a thinner but richer sauce, use egg yolks only.
Beat 4 yolks with a couple of tablespoons of light cream. Use thin strips of ham or prosciutto instead of bacon.

Spaghetti with Red Clam Sauce

Shellfish are very fast cooking, making them a perfect choice for work-a-day meals when time is precious. Though quick to prepare, this dish makes no short cuts in flavor. Fresh herbs, tomatoes and red bell peppers are simmered with white wine and briny clams, creating an elegant and satisfying meal.

2 red bell peppers
3–4 ripe tomatoes
1 lb (500 g) dried spaghetti
1 tablespoon oil
1 medium onion, diced
2 cloves garlic, minced
1 red finger-length chili pepper, finely
  chopped
2 lbs (1 kg) fresh clams, rinsed
$1/4$ cup (60 ml) white wine
1 tablespoon balsamic vinegar
1 tablespoon tomato paste
2 tablespoons chopped fresh oregano

Serves 4

1 Quarter the bell peppers; remove the seeds and membranes. Broil (grill) the peppers, skin side up, until the skin blisters and blackens. Transfer to a paper bag and close. When the peppers are cool enough to handle, peel away the skin. Slice the peppers into thin strips. Cut the tomatoes in half and place under a hot broiler (grill) until lightly browned and softened, 5 to 10 minutes. Set aside.

2 Meanwhile, cook the spaghetti in large pot of boiling salted water until al dente. Drained.

3 Heat the oil in a large saucepan over medium heat. Add the onion, garlic and chili and cook, stirring, until the onion is soft. Add the clams and wine, cover, increase the heat to high and cook, swirling the pan over the heat, for 5 minutes, or until the clams open; discard any that do not open. Stir in the peppers, vinegar, tomato paste and oregano and heat through.

4 Place the drained spaghetti on a serving platter. Serve topped with the clam mixture and dotted with the roasted tomatoes.

Notes:
1. Almost any herb will suit this simple, light dish—try fresh coriander leaves, parsley, fennel, marjoram, thyme and mint leaves.
2. A word or caution—too much chili will spoil the subtle flavors of this dish.

Quick Spaghetti with Tomato Basil Sauce

With an abundance of sweet fresh basil, this light pasta dish offers maximum flavor for minimum time.

2¹/₂ lbs (1.25 kg) ripe tomatoes or two
   14-oz (400-g) cans whole tomatoes
1 clove garlic, peeled and sliced
2 tablespoons oil
2–3 tablespoons chopped fresh basil and
   oregano leaves
1 lb (500 g) dried pasta, cooked until al
   dente, to serve
Chopped fresh basil and oregano leaves,
   to garnish
Parmesan shavings, to garnish

Serves 4

1 If using ripe tomatoes, rinse and place 2 or 3 at a time in a saucepan of simmering water for 30 to 45 seconds, or until the skins begin to break. Remove with a slotted spoon and drain. Use a sharp knife to peel off the skins and remove the cores; discard.
2 Place the tomatoes, in batches, in a blender or food processor and process briefly into coarse chunks.
3 Heat the oil in a large, heavy-based saucepan over medium heat. Add the garlic and stir-fry 1 minute. Add the tomatoes and basil leaves and bring to a boil, stirring constantly. Reduce the heat and simmer for 8 to 10 minutes, or until the sauce thickens. Pour over the hot cooked pasta, sprinkled with basil leaves and Parmesan if desired.

Pasta Shells with Aromatic Meatballs

This special pasta dish combines the flavors of the Middle East with hearty tomato sauce and meatballs.

10 oz (300 g) ground beef
$1/_4$ cup (15 g) fine dry breadcrumbs
2 tablespoons finely chopped pitted olives
1 clove garlic, crushed
$1/_4$ teaspoon ground coriander
$1/_4$ teaspoon ground cumin seeds
1 tablespoon chopped fresh parsley
1 teaspoon finely grated lemon rind
Salt and freshly ground pepper, to taste
8 oz (250 g) dried pasta shells
$2^1/_2$ cups (625 ml) tomato sauce
2 tablespoons finely grated Parmesan
Chopped fresh basil, to garnish

1 Preheat oven to 350°F (180°C).
2 Combine the meat, breadcrumbs, olives, garlic, spices, parsley, lemon rind and salt and pepper in a bowl. Form into $1/_2$-in (12-mm) meatballs. Place on a baking sheet and bake for 10 to 15 minutes.
3 Meanwhile, cook the pasta in large saucepan of boiling salted water until al dente. Drain. Warm the tomato sauce.
4 Serve the meatballs over the hot pasta with the tomato sauce. Sprinkle with Parmesan and basil.

Note: For tastier meatballs, use a combination of 5 oz (150 g) each ground beef and veal or pork.

Serves 2

Quick Pasta with Roasted Eggplant

This dish will win the heart of eggplant and non-eggplant lovers alike.

1 large globe eggplant

Salt, to taste

2 tablespoons oil

1–2 cloves garlic, minced

1 lb (500 g) dried rigatoni or penne pasta

1 cup (250 ml) Italian tomato sauce or pasta
  sauce

$1/2$ cup (100 g) crumbled feta or goat
  cheese

Serves 4

1 Cut the eggplant lengthwise into thin slices. Sprinkle liberally with the salt and let stand for a few minutes to release the juices. Pat dry with paper towels.

2 Place the eggplant slices on a tray under an oven broiler or grill, brush with about 1 tablespoon of olive oil and sprinkle with the garlic. Cook under high heat until very brown, about 15 minutes, turning to cook both sides and brushing occasionally with more oil.

3 Meanwhile, cook the pasta until al dente. Drain, return to the hot saucepan with the tomato sauce and toss.

4 Cut the eggplant into strips and toss through the pasta with the crumbled feta or goat cheese.

Easy Tomato and Tuna Pasta

This delicious recipe calls for commonly stocked ingredients, making it a great back-up dinner.

1 lb (500 g) dried pasta shells, cooked until al dente and drained

1 tablespoon oil

1 medium onion, chopped

6 oz (180 g) canned tuna (water packed), drained

2 tablespoons white wine

14-oz (400-g) can chopped tomatoes, undrained

3/4 cup (180 ml) half-and-half or light cream

3/4 cup (90 g) pitted black olives

2 tablespoons prepared Pesto (page 48)

1 Heat the oil in a saucepan over medium heat. Add the onion and cook, stirring, until soft. Add the tuna, wine, tomatoes and cream and cook over medium heat, stirring occasionally, for 5 minutes or until heated through. Add the olives and Pesto and heat through, stirring.

2 Pour over the cooked pasta and served immediately.

Notes:

1. Other canned fish (salmon or sardines) can be substituted for tuna.
2. The Pesto can also be replaced by 2 cloves of minced garlic and a tablespoon of dried herbs.

Serves 4

Pumpkin, Ricotta and Pesto Pasta

Your family and friends will love this savory pumpkin recipe. Make this pasta dish with fresh pumpkin to expand your repertoire of seasonal recipes and celebrate autumn harvest in an expected way. It can also be made year-round with canned pumpkin.

3$^1/_2$ cups (400 g) fresh pumpkin or acorn
  squash, peeled and cubed, or one 15-oz
  (425-g) can pumpkin puree
1 tablespoon butter
2 tablespoons light cream or milk
Salt and freshly ground pepper, to taste
8 oz (250 g) dried bowtie pasta
$^1/_2$ cup (125 g) ricotta cheese, cubed
1 teaspoon oil

Pesto
1$^1/_2$ cups (60 g) chopped fresh basil leaves
1 clove garlic
$^1/_4$ cup (60 ml) oil
$^1/_4$ cup (30 g) finely grated Parmesan
1 tablespoon toasted pine nuts (see note)

Serves 2

1 To make the Pesto, blend the basil leaves with the garlic in a food processor until the leaves are coarsely chopped. With the motor running, add the oil in a steady stream. Add the Parmesan and pine nuts and process until combined and almost smooth.
2 Steam or boil the pumpkin until tender. Mash, adding the butter, cream, salt and pepper. Keep warm.
3 Meanwhile, cook the pasta in a large saucepan of lightly salted water until al dente.
4 Cut the ricotta cheese into slices $^1/_2$ in (1 cm) thick and arrange on a baking sheet. Brush with a little oil and broil (grill) at medium heat for 3 minutes on each side. Remove and crumble.
5 Drain the pasta. Stir the pumpkin through the cooked pasta and serve immediately topped with the crumbled ricotta cheese and Pesto.

Notes:
1. You can make your own pesto or use a prepared variety. This recipe makes about 1 cup (250 ml), which can be stored in the refrigerator for up to 1 week.
2. Toast the pine nuts by placing them under a broiler (grill) or in a dry pan over medium heat and cook, stirring, until they just change color, 3–4 minutes. Be careful not to burn them.

Tossed Oriental Noodles with Sweet Chili Dressing

Infused with the flavors of fresh ginger or/and coriander leaves, this aromatic noodle dish will satisfy those looking for something new to add to their dinner repertoire. This easy-to-make dish can easily be fortified with the addition of fish or chicken.

10 oz (300 g) dried Chinese egg noodles or
  fettuccine
2 tablespoons oil
2 cups (125 g) snow peas
1 rcd bell pepper
4 oz (125 g) oyster or shiitake mushrooms
4 green onions (scallions) with
1 clove garlic
1 tablespoon grated fresh ginger
1 tablespoon toasted sesame seeds
  (see note)

Sweet Chili Dressing
1 tablespoon chopped coriander leaves
  (cilantro)
2 tablespoons oil
2 tablespoons lime or lemon juice
1 tablespoon bottled sweet chili sauce
1 tablespoon soy sauce

Serves 4

1 To make the Sweet Chili Dressing, place the coriander leaves, oil, lime or lemon juice, chili and soy sauce in a screw-top jar, cover and shake well to blend.

2 Soak the noodles in a bowl of hot water for 10 minutes or until the strands separate. Drain. Cook noodles in a large saucepan of boiling water for 2 to 3 minutes or until al dente. Drain and rinse under cold running water. Drain again and toss with 1 tablespoon of oil.

3 Meanwhile, trim the stem ends from the snow peas. Halve the bell pepper, remove the seeds and cut into thin strips. Thinly slice the mushrooms and green onions. Peel and slice the garlic.

4 Heat the remaining oil in a wok or large, heavy-based frying pan over high heat. Add the garlic and ginger and stir-fry for 1 minute. Add the snow peas and bell pepper and stir-fry for 2 to 3 minutes or until the snow peas turn bright green. Add the mushrooms, green onions, noodles and Dressing and heat through, stirring.

5 Sprinkle the toasted sesame seeds onto the noodles and serve immediately.

Notes:
1. Chinese egg noodles can be purchased in bundles in both fine and thicker widths from oriental food stores and supermarkets. If using wide noodles, cook them for 3 to 5 minutes.
2. Try adding 1–1$\frac{1}{2}$ cups (250 to 350 g) flaked poached fish or finely sliced cooked chicken.
3. Toast the sesame seeds in a frying pan over medium heat until golden brown. Keep moving the pan so the seeds do not burn.

Quick Seafood Paella

Satisfying meal-in-one rice dishes that feature a sumptuous variety of ingredients and seasonings are popular around the world. In this delicious Spanish rice dish, named after the traditional two-handled pan it's prepared in, a medley of seafood, pork sausage, chicken and saffron delight the palate.

2 chicken quarters (breasts with wings or legs with thighs)
2 tablespoons oil
1 onion, peeled and sliced
1 green bell pepper, deseeded and sliced
1 red bell pepper, deseeded and sliced
2 cloves garlic, crushed
14-oz (400-g) can peeled tomatoes
1 small cinnamon stick
Salt and pepper, to taste
$1^3/_4$ cups (400 ml) chicken stock
$1/_4$ teaspoon saffron
2 tablespoons boiling water
$1^1/_3$ cups (285 g) uncooked long-grain rice
4 oz (125 g) peeled shrimp, thawed if frozen
4 oz (125 g) squid rings (calamari), thawed if frozen
$1/_2$ cup (90 g) sliced chorizo sausage
12–16 fresh shrimp, in their shells
$1^1/_4$ cups (180 g) fresh or frozen peas
12–16 large fresh mussels, cleaned

1 Cut the chicken into small pieces, discarding as much of the carcass as possible. Heat the oil in a large frying pan, casserole dish or paella pan and fry the chicken and onion until golden brown.
2 Add the bell peppers and garlic and continue cooking for 2 to 3 minutes, then add the canned tomatoes and their liquid, cinnamon, seasonings and stock, and bring to a boil. Cover and simmer gently for 15 minutes, until the chicken is tender.
3 Mix the saffron with 2 tablespoons boiling water. Add to the pan with the rice and bring back to a boil. Cover and simmer gently for 15 minutes. Stir in the shrimp, squid rings, chorizo, shrimp in shells and peas, and place the mussels on top. Add a little more boiling stock or water if needed. Cover again and simmer for about 10 minutes, or until the rice is tender and all the liquid has been absorbed and the mussel shells have opened. (If any mussels remain closed, discard them.)
4 Serve the paella hot with crusty bread and provide a finger bowl and paper napkins.

Serves 4

Simple Mushroom Risotto

Perfect risotto will have a wonderfully creamy texture while the individual rice grains will be firm—neither mushy nor crunchy. Obtaining this result isn't hard, but it does take patience. The trick is to make sure you stir the rice constantly while it's cooking in the hot stock and to make sure that all of the stock is absorbed before adding more.

1 small onion, diced
1 clove garlic
2 cups (180 g) sliced mushrooms
6 cups (1.4 liters) chicken stock
2 tablespoons butter
2 cups (400 g) uncooked arborio or short-
   grain rice
$1/_2$ cup (60 g) freshly grated Parmesan
Freshly ground black pepper, to taste
Parmesan shavings, to garnish
Chopped fresh parsley, to garnish

Serves 4

1 Peel and slice the garlic. Halve or quarter the mushrooms, if large.
2 Bring the stock to a boil in a saucepan over high heat.
3 Meanwhile, melt the butter in a large, heavy-based saucepan over medium heat. Add the onion, garlic and mushrooms, and cook stirring, for 3 to 5 minutes, or until the liquid from the mushrooms has evaporated. Add the rice and stir until well coated with the butter mixture. Reduce the heat and stir in $1/_2$ cup (125 ml) of the boiling stock. Cook gently, stirring occasionally, until the stock is absorbed.
4 Continue adding more stock and cooking in this way for 25 to 30 minutes or until all the stock is absorbed and the rice is tender but still firm to the bite (al dente).
5 Stir in the grated Parmesan and season to taste with pepper. Serve with the Parmesan shavings and chopped parsley.

Note: When cooked, the risotto should have a creamy consistency; if too stiff, stir in a little extra stock. To make Parmesan shavings, use a swivel-bladed vegetable peeler to cut thin shavings from a large piece of fresh, room-temperature cheese. Serve with a fresh green salad and crusty bread.

Fried Rice with Bacon and Chinese Greens

With its satisfying contrast of tastes and textures, this dish is a delicious way to use leftover rice.

2 teaspoons oil
1 egg, beaten
2 slices bacon, chopped
$1/_2$ cup (50 g) sliced mushrooms
3 green onions (scallions), cut into lengths
1 clove garlic, minced
2 teaspoons grated fresh ginger
3 cups (300 g) cooked long-grain rice
1 tablespoon soy sauce
2 bunches baby bok choy
Salt and freshly ground pepper, to taste
Extra soy sauce, to serve

1 Heat 1 teaspoon of oil in a nonstick frying pan or wok. Add the egg and cook over medium heat until the top begins to bubble. Gently flip the omelet and cook the other side for 1 to 2 minutes. Roll up, remove and chop. Set aside.
2 Heat the remaining oil in a frying pan or wok and cook the bacon, mushrooms, green onions, garlic and ginger over medium heat for 3 to 4 minutes. Add the rice and cook for 3 to 4 more minutes, stirring. Add the soy sauce and chopped omelet.
3 Meanwhile, steam the bok choy until tender, about 5 minutes. Season with a little salt and pepper.
4 Serve the fried rice with the bok choy and extra soy sauce to taste.

Serves 2

Chicken Rice Pilaf

Made with root vegetables, this sunshine-yellow pilaf is the perfect dish to warm a cold winter's day.

2 boneless chicken thigh fillets
1 whole chicken breast
3 teaspoons ground turmeric
2 tablespoons oil
Seeds from 8 cardamom pods
1 small carrot, finely diced
1 small parsnip, finely diced
3 cloves garlic, crushed
1 cup (200 g) uncooked long-grain rice
2 ripe tomatoes, peeled and diced
2 cups (500 ml) chicken stock
2 tablespoons chopped fresh mint, to garnish

Serves 4

1 Toss the chicken with 2 teaspoons ground turmeric in a paper bag. Heat 1 tablespoon of oil in a large frying pan over medium-high heat. Add the chicken and cook, turning occasionally until browned all over. Remove from the pan.

2 Heat the remaining oil in the same pan over medium heat. Add the cardamom, carrot, parsnip and garlic and cook for 5 minutes, being careful not to overcook the garlic. Add the rice and continue cooking for another 5 minutes, stirring frequently.

3 Cut the chicken into bite-size chunks and add to the rice mixture. Add the tomatoes, stock and the remaining ground turmeric. Cover and simmer gently until the rice is cooked through, about 20 minutes. Sprinkle with the mint leaves and serve.

Pan-fried Chicken with Mustard Sauce

This classic French combination of sautéed chicken and mustard sauce is one of our favorite dinners. It's an incredibly fast meal that to be complete need only be served with a vegetable or green salad. We recommend a little crusty French bread on the side to soak up the delicious sauce.

4 boneless chicken breast or $2^1/_2$ lbs
  (1.25 kg) chicken pieces
Freshly ground black pepper, to taste
2 tablespoons butter
1 tablespoon oil

Mustard Sauce
$^1/_2$ cup (125 ml) chicken stock, dry white
  wine or water
2 tablespoons Dijon mustard
1 teaspoon mustard seeds (optional)
$^3/_4$ cup (180 ml) heavy cream

Serves 4

1 Rinse the chicken under cold running water and pat dry with paper towels. Remove the skin and sprinkle with pepper to taste.
2 Heat the butter and oil in a large, heavy-based frying pan over medium heat. When the foaming subsides, add the chicken and cook for 5 to 6 minutes on each side or until golden brown.
3 Cover the pan, reduce the heat and cook for 8 to 10 minutes, or until the chicken is just tender—pieces on the bone take longer than fillets. Using tongs, transfer the chicken to a heated serving platter and cover loosely with foil to keep warm.
4 To make the Mustard Sauce, drain the excess fat from the pan, leaving 1 to 2 tablespoons fat with the cooking juices. Add the stock, mustard and cream to the pan, and mix well over medium heat. Bring to a boil and simmer, stirring occasionally, 5 minutes or until the Sauce reduces and thickens slightly.
5 Pour the Mustard Sauce over the chicken and serve immediately.

Note: Serve this with a Mushroom Sauce in place of Mustard Sauce. To make the Mushroom Sauce, add $1^1/_2$ cups (130 g) sliced mushrooms and cook with the chicken. Use chicken stock instead of wine or water and substitute 2 tablespoons dry sherry for the mustard.

Grilled Chicken with Aromatic Spice Rub

An aromatic spice rub gives grilled chicken great flavor while at the same time sealing in moisture.

2 teaspoons minced ginger
2 cloves garlic, minced
1 teaspoon salt
$^1/_2$ teaspoon ground black pepper
1 teaspoon ground cumin
1 teaspoon paprika
2 teaspoons ground coriander
2 tablespoons coriander leaves (cilantro),
  chopped (optional)
2 tablespoons lemon juice
3 tablespoons oil
2 whole chicken breasts or 4 halves,
  skin removed

1 Combine the spices, juice and oil to make a paste. Rub into the chicken and let stand in the refrigerator for at least 30 minutes or longer for better flavor.
2 Heat a broiler (grill) or grill pan and cook the chicken for about 5 minutes each side, until cooked through. Serve hot or chilled.

Note: You can also cut the meat into bite-size chunks and thread them onto skewers before grilling. The chicken can also be roasted rather than grilled, although this is best done with a half or whole chicken. It takes longer but is hassle-free. Place in a baking dish and cook in a preheated 350°F (180°C) oven for about 45 minutes.

Serves 2

Stuffed Chicken Breasts Wrapped in Prosciutto

Calling for just a handful of ingredients, this recipe enables you to create an elegant dinner on the fly.

4 boneless chicken breasts
8 slices of camembert cheese (about 4 oz/125 g)
2 teaspoons fresh thyme
8 thin slices prosciutto ham
2 tablespoons oil
8 green onions (scallions), finely chopped
$^1/_4$ cup (60 ml) dry white wine
$^1/_2$ cup (125 ml) heavy cream

Note: Camembert is a soft, creamy French cheese. If unavailable, substitute brie or Italian paglietta.

1 Cut a few shallow slits into the sides of the chicken breasts and stuff each breast with 2 slices of the cheese. Sprinkle the fillets with thyme, wrap with the prosciutto and secure with toothpicks.
2 Heat the oil in a large frying pan over medium heat. Add the chicken fillets and cook until tender and lightly browned, about 10 minutes on each side. Remove the chicken from the pan and keep warm.
3 Return the pan to the heat. Add the green onions to the juices and cook, stirring, until soft. Add the wine and cream and simmer until heated through and slightly thickened, about 5 minutes. Serve the chicken drizzled with the sauce.

Serves 4

Creamy Chicken Kiev

Traditional chicken Kiev, which takes its name from the capital city of Ukraine, consists of a pounded chicken fillet rolled around a chilled piece of butter. Our quick-and-easy version forgoes the pounding and rolling process, but retains all the great flavor of the famous dish.

4 boneless chicken breasts
2 tablespoons oil
2 onions, peeled and thinly sliced
1 red bell pepper, deseeded and sliced
1 green bell pepper, deseeded and sliced
$1^1/_2$ cups (125 g) sliced mushrooms
2 tablespoons fresh thyme leaves
4 tablespoons stock or white wine
Salt and pepper, to taste
$2/_3$ cup (150 ml) sour cream or yogurt
Freshly chopped parsley, to garnish

1 Cut the chicken into strips. Heat half the oil in a nonstick pan and fry the pieces briskly until lightly browned and cooked through. Remove from the pan.

2 Put the rest of the oil in the pan, add the onions and fry gently until soft, about 7 to 8 minutes. Add the bell peppers and cook gently for 3 to 4 minutes; then add the mushrooms and continue cooking for a further 2 to 3 minutes.

3 Return the chicken to the pan with the herbs, stock and seasonings, bring to a boil and simmer for 2 to 3 minutes. Stir in the sour cream and reheat gently.

4 Adjust the seasonings and serve sprinkled with plenty of chopped parsley on a bed of boiled rice or pasta.

Serves 4

Baked Chicken Fingers with Tartar Sauce

Our healthy baked chicken fingers are easy to make and are always a hit with kids.

4 boneless chicken breasts
$^1/_2$ cup (75 g) all-purpose (plain) flour
1–2 eggs, beaten
Golden or dry breadcrumbs
1 cup (250 ml) mayonnaise
1 scant tablespoon chopped capers
2 tablespoons pickle relish or 2 gherkins, diced
8 stuffed green olives, finely chopped
1 clove garlic, crushed (optional)
2 tablespoons chopped chives
1 tablespoon freshly chopped parsley
Finely grated rind of $^1/_4$ lemon or $^1/_2$ lime
Lemon or lime wedges, to serve

1 Preheat the oven to 375°F (190°C). Remove the skin from the chicken and cut the chicken into long, narrow strips. Coat the strips lightly in the flour then dip into the beaten egg and coat with the breadcrumbs. Chill until ready to cook.
2 Combine the mayonnaise, capers, gherkins, olives, garlic, chives, parsley and lemon rind, adding seasonings to taste. Place in a bowl, cover and let stand for at least an hour before serving.
3 Bake the chicken in the oven for 20 to 30 minutes, turning once, until golden brown and crisp.
4 Serve hot or cold, garnished with lemon or lime quarters or wedges and watercress or parsley.

Serves 4

Simple Coq Au Vin

A French version of chicken-in-a-pot, Coq Au Vin is a classic wintertime crowd pleaser.

1 tablespoon oil
5 boneless chicken thighs, skin removed
  and cut into bite-size pieces
$^1/_2$ small leek, sliced
1 small carrot, sliced
1 celery stalk, sliced
1 cup (100 g) mushrooms
1 cup (250 ml) dry white wine
1 cup (250 ml) chicken stock
Salt and freshly ground pepper, to taste
1 tablespoon chopped fresh parsley
Cooked noodles or rice, to serve

1 Heat 2 teaspoons of oil in a saucepan and brown the chicken pieces on all sides over medium heat, about 2 to 3 minutes. Remove and set aside.
2 Heat the remaining oil. Add the leek, carrot, celery and mushrooms and cook over low heat, partially covered, for 5 minutes, stirring occasionally.
3 Return the chicken to the pan with the wine and stock. Bring to a boil, reduce the heat and simmer for 15 to 20 minutes.
4 Season to taste with salt and pepper and stir in the chopped parsley. Serve with the hot noodles or rice.

Serves 2

Fragrant Chicken Curry with Toasted Almonds

Curry recipes often have a daunting list of ingredients—the bulk of which are aromatic spices and fresh herbs that give curries their deeply complex and satisfying flavor. At first glance, you may be put off by the number of ingredients. Don't be. Often it's as simple as assembling jars of spice from your cupboard and adding them to meat or vegetables. And the results are always worth it! For variety, try serving this dish with Fresh Potato Curry with Peas (page 28) in place of or along with rice or couscous.

1 chicken, cut into pieces
$1/4$ cup (45 g) all-purpose (plain) flour
$3/4$ teaspoon salt
$1/4$ teaspoon freshly ground black pepper
$1/4$ teaspoon paprika
1 clove garlic
1 small onion
1 green bell pepper
$1/4$ cup ($1/2$ stick/60 g) butter
2 teaspoons curry powder or curry paste
$1/2$ teaspoon dried thyme
14-oz (400-g) can crushed tomatoes, undrained
3 tablespoons chopped seedless raisins
3 tablespoons chopped fresh parsley or coriander leaves (cilantro)
$1/4$ cup (40 g) sliced almonds, pan-roasted (see note)
Cooked rice or couscous, to serve
Fruit chutney, to serve

Serves 4–6

1 Rinse the chicken pieces under cold running water and dry with paper towels.
2 Place the flour, salt, pepper and paprika in a paper bag or container. Place 1 or 2 chicken pieces at a time into the bag, seal and shake to coat.
3 Peel and finely chop the garlic and onion. Halve the bell pepper, remove the seeds and cut into $1/4$-in (6-mm) dice.
4 Melt the butter in a large, heavy frying pan over medium heat. Add the chicken, in batches, and cook for 1 to 2 minutes each side or until brown. Transfer the cooked chicken to a plate. Drain the excess fat from the pan, leaving 1 to 2 tablespoons of fat with the cooking juices.
5 Add the garlic, onion and bell pepper to the pan and sauté over medium heat for 3 to 5 minutes, until the onion is golden. Add the remaining ingredients except the chicken and almonds and bring to a simmer.
6 Return the chicken to the pan and cover. Reduce the heat and simmer gently for 20 to 30 minutes until the chicken is tender.
7 Just before serving, roast the almonds in a dry, nonstick frying pan over medium heat, stirring until brown.
8 Serve the chicken on rice or couscous, sprinkled with the toasted almonds and accompanied by the fruit chutney.

Note: Toast the almonds by placing them in a dry frying pan over medium heat, and fry until lightly browned, stirring constantly, for 3–4 minutes. Be careful not to burn.

Chinese Stir-fry with Chicken and Cashews

Just three ingredients—tender chicken, crisp celery and meaty cashews—give this classic stir-fry great taste and texture.

2 tablespoons oil
1 cup (125 g) raw cashew nuts
1 bunch green onions (scallions), trimmed and sliced
4–5 sticks celery, sliced diagonally
4 boneless chicken breasts, skinned and cut into $1/_2$-in (12-mm) cubes
$3/_4$ cup (180 ml) yellow bean sauce or miso
1 teaspoon sugar, or to taste
Salt and pepper, to taste
Cooked rice, to serve

1 Using a wok or a heavy-based saucepan or skillet, heat the oil until it smokes. Toss in the cashew nuts, green onions and celery and cook for 1 to 2 minutes, stirring frequently over a medium-high heat until the nuts are lightly browned.
2 Add the chicken and cook quickly, stirring frequently for 2 to 3 minutes until the juices are sealed in and just cooked. Add the yellow bean sauce or miso, and sugar. Season lightly with salt and pepper and cook for a further minute or so, until piping hot. Serve immediately with hot rice.

Serves 4

Chicken with Honey Lemon Sauce

This unusual dish—made with honey, citrus and nuts—conjures the exotic flavors of ancient Persia.

4 boneless chicken breasts
3 tablespoons butter
$^3/_4$ cup (180 ml) white wine
$^1/_3$ cup (80 ml) chicken stock
1 tablespoon lemon juice
1 teaspoon rind of tangerine, clementine or
  tangelo
Salt and pepper, to taste
1 tangerine, clementine or tangelo
$^1/_2$ cup (60 g) walnut halves, crushed
$1^1/_2$ tablespoons honey
1 tablespoon cornstarch
2 tablespoons brandy
Watercress, to serve

1 Remove any skin from the chicken pieces and season lightly. Heat the butter in a pan and fry the chicken gently for about 3 minutes until golden brown and almost cooked through. Add the wine, stock, lemon juice, tangerine rind and seasonings. Bring to a boil.
2 Peel and cut the tangerine into segments, leaving the membrane behind, and remove any seeds. Add segments to the pan with the walnuts and honey. Simmer, covered, for 8 to 10 minutes, until tender. Thicken the sauce with the cornstarch blended in a little cold water, bring back to a boil and simmer for a minute or so.
3 Pour the brandy over the chicken and ignite. Adjust the seasoning.
4 Serve each portion of chicken with the sauce spooned over. Garnish with a sprig of watercress.

Serves 4

Cajun Chicken with Rémoulade Sauce

A little spice livens any evening, and this recipe for Cajun chicken fingers and creamy Rémoulade Sauce is truly lip smacking good. Rémoulade is essentially French tartar sauce with a lot more going on than its English cousin. Cajuns transformed the original French recipe for Rémoulade to come up with a unique spicy version that we love.

1$^1/_4$ cups (180 g) all-purpose (plain) flour
2 tablespoons Cajun spice mix (see note)
2 teaspoons dried marjoram
1 teaspoon dried sage
1$^1/_2$ teaspoons salt
$^1/_4$ teaspoon ground black pepper
1 egg
1 cup (250 ml) milk
$^1/_4$ cup (60 ml) light cream
6 boneless chicken breasts, skinned and cut into long, narrow strips
Oil, for deep-frying

Rémoulade Sauce
1 egg
$^1/_4$ cup (60 g) wholegrain mustard
1 teaspoon Cajun spice mix (see note)
$^1/_4$ cup (25 g) chopped green onions (scallions)
$^1/_4$ cup (15 g) chopped parsley
1 teaspoon Worcestershire sauce
$^1/_4$–$^1/_2$ teaspoon hot sauce
1 teaspoon salt
1 cup (250 ml) oil

Serves 6

1 To make the Rémoulade Sauce, combine the egg, mustard, spice mix, green onions, parsley, Worcestershire sauce, Tabasco and salt in a blender or food processor and pulse once or twice to mix thoroughly. With the machine running, add the oil in a slow, steady stream, blending until the Sauce is smooth and creamy. Taste for salt and Tabasco and pour into a bowl. Refrigerate the Sauce until ready to serve.
2 Mix the flour, spice mix, marjoram, sage, salt and pepper in a deep plate.
3 Beat the egg with the milk and cream in a shallow dish or pie plate.
4 Soak the chicken pieces in the milk mixture for 10 to 15 minutes, turning the pieces occasionally so that all are well coated.
5 Dredge the chicken in the seasoned flour and shake off any excess.
6 Pour the oil into a deep frying pan and heat over high heat (a little flour sprinkled on top of the oil should sizzle at the right temperature). Fry the chicken over medium-high heat, turning often, for 10 to 15 minutes, or until deep golden brown. Do not burn the chicken. Drain on paper towels.
7 Serve the chicken immediately with the Rémoulade Sauce.

Note:
1. To make Cajun spice mix, combine $^1/_2$ cup (60 g) paprika, $^1/_4$ cup (30 g) black pepper, 1$^1/_2$ tablespoons cayenne pepper, 2 tablespoons garlic powder, 2 tablespoons onion powder and store in a closed jar in a cool, dry place. Use within a month for maximum flavor.
2. Rémoulade Sauce will last for up to a week in the refrigerator. If you prefer not to eat raw egg, omit the oil and the egg and replace with 1 cup (250 ml) mayonnaise.

Perfect Steaks

A juicy grilled steak cooked to your liking is always delicious—the aroma alone brings everyone to the table! And steaks are also quick cooking—particularly if you enjoy them rare or medium-rare—making them a great option when time is short. For a balanced meal, serve with grilled vegetables.

2 large potatoes, peeled, sliced into $1/4$-in (6-mm) rounds

1 red bell pepper, deseeded and cut into 1-in (2.5-cm) thick slices

1 eggplant, cut into 1/2-in (1.25 cm) thick slices

1 zucchini, cut on the diagonal into $1/2$-in (12-mm) slices

Oil

Salt

Freshly ground black pepper

4 tender steaks e.g. T-bone, sirloin, porter-house, rib-eye or New York strip (shown on facing page), cut about 1 in (2.5 cm) thick

Savory Butter Topping (Optional)

$1/2$ cup (1 stick/125 g) soft butter

Seasonings:

1 to 2 tablespoons hot English mustard, horseradish relish or chili sauce

2 to 3 teaspoons grated lemon rind

2 finely chopped garlic cloves

2 to 3 tablespoons chopped fresh herb, such as mint, basil, sage, rosemary, dill, chives, or a combination

Serves 4

1 To serve steaks with the Savory Butter Topping, beat the butter until creamy with one or more of the Savory Butter seasonings. Roll the seasoned butter into a log form, cover with plastic wrap, and place in the freezer briefly or refrigerator until chilled.

2 Heat a charcoal grill until the coals are ash-covered and glowing, or preheat an oven broiler or grill to medium-high heat. Place cooking rack about 4 in (10 cm) away from heat.

3 Parboil the potatoes slices and let cool. Brush the vegetables with oil to lightly coat and season with salt and pepper.

4 Trim any excess fat from the steaks and sprinkle with salt and pepper. Brush the rack with oil to prevent the meat from sticking.

5 Place the vegetables and steaks on the rack. Sear the steaks for 30 to 45 seconds on each side. Reduce the heat slightly (or move the steaks from the hot part of the grill) and continue to cook, turning once only, for 4 to 5 minutes each side, or until done as desired. Use tongs to test steak for doneness—rare steak feels soft and red juices puddle on the surface; medium is firm but pliable and juices are still pink; well-done is firm, stiff and dry-looking.

6 Cook the vegetables until they are lightly charred and tender, about 8 minutes, turning once or twice while cooking.

7 Serve the vegetables and steak immediately. Serve the steak with slices of chilled Savory Butter Topping over top, if using.

Note: Whether barbecued or grilled, the rule is the same: sear meat quickly on both sides to seal in the juices, then reduce the heat and cook as desired. This also applies to chops, whether lamb, pork or veal.

Lamb Chops with Creamy White Beans

For a perfect pairing, serve this rich yet subtle dish with a fresh watercress salad.

2 teaspoons oil
1 clove garlic, minced
2 thin slices Canadian bacon, cut into strips
14-oz (400-g) cannellini beans, rinsed and
  drained
6 fresh sage leaves
2 teaspoons fresh thyme leaves
Salt and freshly ground pepper, to taste
$^1/_4$ cup (60 ml) light cream
4 lamb chops, trimmed
$^1/_4$ cup (30 g) shaved Parmesan, to serve

1 Heat the oil in a frying pan over medium heat. Add the garlic and Canadian bacon and cook, 2 to 3 minutes. Add the beans and cook for 2 to 3 more minutes. Add the herbs, salt, pepper and cream and heat through, about 2 minutes.
2 Meanwhile, pan-fry or grill the lamb for 4 to 5 minutes on each side for medium.
3 Serve the lamb with the beans sprinkled with Parmesan.

Note: Instead of lamb, try grilled tuna steaks—cook them 3 minutes on each side for medium-rare.

Serves 2

Grilled Lamb Chops with Pesto Sauce

This elegant and flavorful recipe is a great addition to your standard grilling repertoire.

2 cloves garlic, crushed and mashed with a
  pinch of salt
2 tablespoons toasted pine nuts
2 cups (60 g) fresh basil leaves
$^1/_2$ cup (60 g) grated Parmesan
5 tablespoons extra virgin olive oil
4 lamb chops
Oil, for brushing
Freshly ground black pepper, to taste

Serves 2

1 Process the pine nuts, basil and Parmesan in a blender or food processor with 1 tablespoon of the olive oil. Add the garlic. With the motor running, pour in the remaining oil in a steady stream so the pesto becomes a smooth paste.
2 Heat a charcoal grill until the coals are ash-covered and glowing, or preheat an oven broiler or grill to medium-high. Place the cooking rack about 4 in (10 cm) away from heat.
3 Trim any excess fat from the lamb and sprinkle with black pepper to taste. Brush the rack with oil to prevent the meat from sticking. Cook the lamb for 30 to 45 seconds each side. Reduce the heat slightly (or move the lamb away from the hot part of the grill) and cook, turning once only, for 4 to 5 minutes each side, or until cooked as desired. Serve immediately with the pesto sauce.

Quick Beef Kebabs

These Greek-inspired kebabs are fast cooking and delicious. Serve with rice or flat bread.

1/2 cup (125 ml) olive oil
Juice of 1 lemon
1 tablespoon chopped fresh oregano
1 tablespoon chopped fresh thyme
Salt and freshly ground black pepper,
  to taste
1 1/2 lbs (700 g) steak, cut into cubes
12 cherry tomatoes
4 long metal skewers or 8 bamboo skewers
  (soaked for 1 hour)

1 Mix together the olive oil, lemon juice, oregano, thyme, salt and pepper in a ceramic or glass bowl. Add the cubed steak and mix well. Cover and chill for at least 30 minutes, or overnight.
2 Remove the meat from the bowl, reserving the marinade.
3 Preheat an oven broiler or grill to high. Divide the meat and tomatoes among kebab skewers, beginning and ending with steak. Grill the skewers for about 5 minutes, turning and brushing with the reserved marinade from time to time.
4 Serve immediately.

Serves 4

Irish Lamb Stew

This hearty stew, with tender pieces of lamb, is a good choice for a fall or winter's day.

1¹/₂ lbs (700 g) boneless lamb, cubed
2 tablespoons all-purpose (plain) flour
Salt and ground black pepper, to taste
2 tablespoons oil
1 tablespoon butter
1 large onion, peeled and chopped
4 strips bacon, chopped
2 cups (500 ml) beef stock
2 carrots, peeled and sliced
8 baby onions, peeled and halved
6 oz (180 g) mushrooms, halved
¹/₂ cup (75 g) fresh or frozen peas
1 teaspoon dried thyme or majoram

1 Place the flour and salt and pepper in a paper bag. Add the meat, seal and shake until the cubes are evenly coated.
2 Heat the oil and butter in a deep, heavy-based frying pan over medium heat until the foaming subsides. Add the meat in batches and cook, turning frequently, until brown on all sides. Use a slotted spoon to transfer the cooked meat to a plate.
3 Add the onion and bacon to the pan and cook, stirring, over medium heat for 5 minutes, or until soft. Return the meat to the pan with the stock, vegetables and thyme and bring to a boil, stirring. Reduce the heat, partially cover and simmer for 1 hour, or until the meat is almost tender and the sauce thickens slightly.

Serves 4

Moroccan Lamb with Couscous or Rice

Moroccan cooking—one of the great cuisines of the world—is characterized by its adept use of aromatic spices, hot peppers for heat, nuts, and dried fruits. Honey is also a common ingredient. This delicious dish captures the flavors of Moroccan cooking without spending hours in the kitchen. Lamb, a popular meat in Morocco, is marinated in a spice blend, quickly sautéed and placed on a bed of fast cooking couscous.

12 lamb chops
1 teaspoon ground coriander
1 teaspoon ground cinnamon
1 teaspoon ground cumin
3 tablespoons chopped fresh parsley
2 tablespoons honey
$1^1/_4$ cups (250 g) dried couscous or 2 cups
  (400 g) uncooked rice
1 tablespoon butter
1 cup (250 ml) boiling water (for couscous)
$3^1/_2$ cups (825 ml) water (for rice)
2 tomatoes, diced
1 hothouse (English) cucumber, deseeded
  and diced
1 teaspoon paprika
3 tablespoons oil

Serves 4

1 Trim the fat from the lamb chops. Combine the ground coriander, cinnamon, cumin, 1 tablespoon parsley and honey in a medium bowl. Add the lamb and coat with the mixture on all sides.

2 To make the couscous, combine the couscous and butter in a medium bowl. Pour the boiling water over the couscous and stir briefly to combine. Cover with plastic wrap for 3 minutes, then gently stir with a fork until the grains are separated and lightly fluffed. Let cool.

3 If you're using rice, rinse the rice in a strainer under cold water until the water runs clear. Combine the rice and water in a heavy-based saucepan and bring to a boil, stirring. Reduce the heat, cover tightly and simmer gently for 12 minutes. Remove from the heat and let stand, covered, for 10 minutes. Fluff the rice with a fork.

4 Stir in the tomatoes, cucumber, remaining 2 tablespoons of parsley and paprika into the fluffed couscous or rice and set aside.

5 Heat the oil in a frying pan and brown the marinated lamb in batches, 2 minutes on each side. Serve the lamb on the bed of couscous or rice salad.

Note: This lamb is best cooked medium-rare, but if you prefer, it can be cooked longer. Chicken thighs make a good alternative—use eight trimmed thigh fillets. When buying couscous, make sure you choose the precooked variety. If hothouse cucumbers are unavailable, any small cucumber will suffice.

Mongolian Lamb

This famous dish is a favorite among spicy-food lovers, yet the amount of heat can easily be adjusted.

$1^1/_2$ lbs (700 g) boneless lamb loin
3–4 cloves garlic, minced
2 tablespoons rice wine or sake
$2^1/_2$ tablespoons sesame oil
1 tablespoon dark soy sauce
1 tablespoon light soy sauce
3 teaspoons sugar
2 teaspoons cornstarch
2 tablespoons oil
1 large onion, finely sliced
1 tablespoon toasted sesame seeds (pg 50)
2 green onions (scallions) tops, shredded
1 red finger-length chili pepper, deseeded
  and thinly sliced

1 Cut the lamb into thin slices, stack several slices together at a time and slice crosswise into very fine shreds. Place in a dish and add the garlic, wine, sesame oil, soy sauces, sugar and cornstarch. Mix well and marinate for at least 30 minutes.
2 Heat frying pan and add the oil. Stir-fry the onion until lightly browned, then push to the side of the pan. Add the meat, reserving the marinade, if any. Cook on a very high heat, stirring and turning continually until the meat is well cooked and very aromatic. Stir in the onions and reserved marinade. Turn off the heat.
3 The dish can be served directly from the pan into bowls of steamed white rice and garnished with the sesame seeds, green onions and chili.

Serves 4

Braised Pork Chops with Herbs

Braising is a great way to achieve flavorful and tender meat. Serve with mashed potatoes or rice.

8–10 pork chops
Freshly ground black pepper, to taste
2 tablespoons oil or butter
1 onion, peeled and diced
1 stalk celery, sliced
$^3/_4$ cup (180 ml) water, stock or dry wine
$^1/_2$ teaspoon dried herbs (such as thyme, sage or rosemary
1 tablespoon cornstarch mixed with 2 tablespoons cold water
Salt and pepper, to taste
2–3 tablespoons chopped parsley, to garnish

Serves 4

1 Trim the excess fat from the chops and sprinkle with pepper.
2 Heat the oil in a large frying pan and cook the chops for 2 to 3 minutes each side. Transfer the chops to a plate and drain the excess fat from the pan, leaving 1 to 2 tablespoons with the cooking juices.
3 Add the onion and celery and sauté over medium heat for 5 minutes until golden. Add the liquid and herbs and bring to a simmer. Return the chops to the pan, reduce the heat, cover and simmer for 20 minutes or until tender, turning once. Transfer to a serving plate and keep warm in the oven.
4 Add the cornstarch mixture to the pan. Cook, stirring constantly, until the sauce boils and thickens. Season with salt and pepper. Pour the sauce over the chops, sprinkle with parsley and serve immediately.

Pork Cutlets with Zesty Tomato Sauce

If you're tired of preparing bland pork cutlets, try this recipe for tender cutlets served with a wonderfully spicy sauce. To double the heat, add some Cajun spice to the breading mix for the cutlets. Remember to slash a few cuts along the edges of the cutlet, particularly where there may any remaining fat, to keep the cutlet from curling up as it cooks. This tip applies to all cutlets and chops.

8 pork cutlets, $1/2$ in (1 cm) thick
1 tablespoon Cajun spice mix (page 70, optional)
1 cup (150 g) all-purpose (plain) flour
2 eggs
1 teaspoon dried marjoram
1 teaspoon salt
$1/4$ teaspoon ground black pepper
1 cup (60 g) fine cracker crumbs or dry breadcrumbs
$3/4$ cup (180 ml) oil

Zesty Tomato Sauce
$1/4$ cup (60 ml) oil
1 onion, peeled and finely diced
6 cloves garlic, minced
1 bell pepper, finely diced
1–2 red finger-length chili peppers, deseeded and minced
20-oz (600-g) can whole peeled tomatoes
1 teaspoon dried thyme and dried marjoram
2 bay leaves
2 tablespoons Cajun spice mix (page 70)

1 Trim the fat from the pork cutlets and flatten them slightly with the side of a cleaver. Slash the edges in two or three places so they won't curl up when frying.

2 Using three pie plates or flat bowls, blend the spice mix (if using) and flour in one; beat the eggs with 1 teaspoon water in another; and mix the majoram, salt, pepper and crumbs in the third (omit salt if using salted crackers for crumbs).

3 To make the Zesty Tomato Sauce, heat the oil in a saucepan over medium heat and stir-fry the onion, garlic, bell peppers and chili peppers. Stir occasionally, until the onion is soft and translucent, about 3–5 minutes. Add the chopped canned tomatoes, with their juicies and the rest of the ingredients.

4 Heat the oil to 350°F (180°C) in a large frying pan. Dip both sides of each cutlet first in the seasoned flour, then in the egg and then in the crumbs. Fry in the hot oil for 3 to 5 minutes on each side or until brown and crisp. Drain on paper towels. Serve with the Zesty Tomato Sauce spooned over the cutlets. Cook for 10 to 15 minutes, or until slightly thickened. Remove from the heat and keep warm.

Serves 4

Beef Fajitas with Two Salsas

This popular Mexican dish is great party fare—each person has fun assembling tortilla wraps to their liking.

1 clove garlic, sliced

1 large onion, sliced

1 large red bell pepper, deseeded and sliced

1 large green bell pepper, deseeded and
  sliced

1 hot pepper, chopped, or 1 teaspoon hot
  chili sauce

2 tablespoons oil

$1^1/_2$ lbs (700 g) steak

Juice of 1 lime

Flour tortillas, sour cream and shredded
  lettuce, to serve

Three Tomato Salsa

1 teaspoon crushed coriander seeds

1 small red onion, diced

2 red tomatoes, diced

2 yellow tomatoes, diced

$^1/_2$ cup (125 g) sun-dried tomatoes in oil,
  drained and chopped

1 tablespoon oil from sun-dried tomatoes

1–2 teaspoons hot pepper sauce

1 tablespoon chopped coriander leaves
  (cilantro)

Avocado Salsa

1 ripe avocado

2 tablespoons sour cream

1 clove garlic, crushed

1 tablespoon lime juice

2–3 drops hot sauce

Salt and freshly ground black pepper, to taste

Grated rind of 1 lime

1 To make the Three Tomato Salsa, combine the coriander seeds, onion, tomatoes, oil, pepper sauce and coriander leaves in a bowl. Mix well and transfer to a serving dish.

2 To make the Avocado Salsa, mash the avocado with the sour cream. Stir in the garlic, lime juice, Tabasco sauce, salt and pepper. Transfer to a serving dish and sprinkle the lime rind over the top.

3 To make the beef fajitas, first cut the beef into thin strips. In a large frying pan or wok stir-fry the garlic, onion, bell peppers and hot pepper and beef in the oil for 2 to 3 minutes until the beef is cooked through. Stir in the lime juice, salt and pepper. Transfer to a warm serving dish and serve with the flour tortillas, sour cream, shredded lettuce and the two Salsas.

Serves 4

Beef and Tofu Sukiyaki

Possibly more liked outside of Japan than in it—the Japanese call this dish "friendship dish" because of its popularity with foreigners—Sukiyaki is normally prepared at the table, making it a fun food to share with a small or large groups. Made with noodles, vegetables, meat and tofu, this hearty dish is a complete meal-in-one.

2 tablespoons mirin (Japanese sweet sake, see note)

2 tablespoons sake or rice wine

2 tablespoons soy sauce

1 tablespoon instant dashi soup stock powder (see note)

1 teaspoon brown sugar

1 cup (250 ml) water

4 tablespoons oil, for frying

$1^1/_4$ lbs (600 g) steak, cut into very thin slices

6–8 fresh shiitake mushrooms, cleaned and sliced

2–3 young leeks, thinly sliced to yield $1^1/_2$ cups

2 cups (180 g) shredded Chinese (Napa) cabbage

4 cups (200 g) bean sprouts

1 cake (8 oz/250 g) firm tofu, cubed

Handful of dried shirataki noodles or glass noodles, blanched in boiling water and drained (see note)

Individual bowls of cooked Japanese rice, to serve

Serves 4

1 Mix together the mirin, sake, soy sauce, dashi powder, sugar and water in a small pan, and bring to a boil. Transfer to a small jug and set aside.

2 Heat the oil in a frying pan. Add the beef, vegetables, tofu and noodles to the pan and stir-fry quickly until the meat is cooked. Transfer to a warmed serving dish and serve immediately with the mirin sauce and rice.

Note:

Sukiyaki is traditionally cooked at the table in either an electric frying pan or a heavy frying pan set over a burner, with each guest cooking their individual portions. Arrange the beef, vegetables, tofu and noodles attractively on serving dishes and serve a bowl of rice for each individual. Heat 1 tablespoon of oil in a frying pan and add a quarter of the beef, stir-fry quickly and transfer to the rice bowls. Then add a quarter of the vegetables, tofu and noodles to the pan and cook quickly, moistening with a little sauce. Transfer to the bowls.

Mirin is a type of sweetened rice wine sold in bottles in Japanese stores. It is used only for cooking—the alcohol dissipates through cooking. Use 1 teaspoon sugar added to 2 teaspoons sake as a substitute for 1 tablespoon mirin.

Dashi powder is used to make dashi fish stock and as a basic seasoning in many soups and salad dressings. It may be substituted with soup stock powder or bouillon cubes.

Shirataki noodles are thin strings of konnyaku, a glutinous paste obtained from the starchy elephant foot plant. They are eaten in sukiyaki and other hotpots. Substitute glass noodles.

Baked Fish with Fresh Tomatoes and Basil

Italian in inspiration, this simple preparation for breaded and baked fish is subtly accented with Parmesan cheese, pine nuts and a touch of garlic. An anchovy fillet adds a depth of flavor that will be appreciated by all—even those who swear they don't like anchovies! The bright flavor of fresh tomato and sweet basil pairs perfectly with the slightly rich fish.

$3/_4$ cup (45 g) fresh breadcrumbs (see note)
1 tablespoon cold butter
2 tablespoons freshly grated Parmesan
2 teaspoons toasted pine nuts (see note)
1 clove garlic
Salt and freshly ground pepper, to taste
10 oz (300 g) firm white fish fillets

Salad
2 teaspoons oil
2 ripe tomatoes, sliced
Salt and freshly ground pepper, to taste
2 tablespoons torn fresh basil leaves
1 teaspoon balsamic vinegar

Serves 2

1 Preheat oven to 400°F (200°C).
2 To prepare the Salad, combine the oil and tomatoes in a bowl. Season with salt and pepper and let stand until ready to serve.
3 Combine the first six ingredients in a food processor and blend until just combined and the mixture resembles coarse crumbs. It is important not to overprocess the coating ingredients—they will stick together if you do. The butter needs to be very cold to ensure a coarsely textured crumb. Gently pat the mixture over each fish fillet. Arrange the fish fillets on a lightly oiled baking sheet. Bake until the topping is crisp and golden, 15 to 20 minutes.
4 To serve, sprinkle the basil and balsamic vinegar over the tomatoes. Spoon onto plates with the fish.

Notes:
1. To make fresh breadcrumbs, remove the crusts from white bread, cut into cubes and process in batches in a food processor until crumbed. Day-old bread works best.
2. Toast the pine nuts by placing them under a broiler (grill) or in a dry pan over medium heat and fry, stirring, until they just change color, 3–4 minutes. Be careful not to burn them.

Pan-fried Fish with Snow Peas and Almonds

In this easy-to-make recipe, a tempting butter-wine sauce with almonds is poured over top crispy pan-fried fish, making this dish ideal for both fancy occasions and weekday dinners. Serve plain white rice or mashed potatoes.

6 tablespoons butter
1$^1/_2$ lbs (700 g) fish fillets
$^1/_2$ cup (75 g) slivered almonds
2 green onions (scallions), chopped
3 cups (200 g) snow peas, steamed
2 tablespoons dry white wine
Salt and freshly ground pepper, to taste

Serves 4

1 Melt 2 tablespoons of the butter in a frying pan over medium heat. Add the fish and cook for 2 to 3 minutes per side, or until the fish is opaque and beginning to flake when tested. Remove and keep warm.
2 Add the almonds to the pan juices and cook over medium heat until golden, about 1 to 2 minutes. Stir in the remaining butter, green onions, snow peas, wine, salt and pepper. Stir until the sauce boils and thickens slightly.
3 To serve, place the fillets on a serving platter and pour the sauce over the top.

Scallops on the Half Shell with Garlic Basil Butter

The naturally rich sweet taste of scallops calls for little embellishment. In this simple recipe, fresh scallops are cooked right in their shells for an elegant presentation. If you can't find scallops on the half shell at the seafood counter, buy the freshest scallops you can find and buy the shells separately.

24 fresh scallops on the half shell
3 tablespoons butter
2 cloves garlic, chopped
3 tablespoons finely chopped leek
3 tablespoons finely chopped fresh basil
Salt and freshly ground pepper, to taste

Serves 4

1 Preheat an oven broiler or grill on high. Arrange the scallops on a tray.
2 Melt the butter in a frying pan over medium heat. Add the garlic and leek and stir-fry for 1 minute, or until tender. Remove from the heat and stir in the basil.
3 Divide the sauce evenly among the scallops; season with salt and pepper. Place under the broiler for 1 to 2 minutes, or until the scallops are opaque. Serve immediately.

Note: This recipe also works well with oysters on the half shell.

Simple Shrimp Risotto

The combination of creamy risotto and tender, just-cooked shrimp make this simple dish one of our favorites.

3 tablespoons butter

3 green onions (scallions), chopped

1 cup (200 g) uncooked arborio or short-grain rice

3 cups (750 ml) chicken or fish stock

Pinch of saffron threads

1 tablespoon oil

10 oz (300 g) uncooked peeled shrimp

2 teaspoons grated lemon rind

1 tablespoon chopped fresh parsley

Salt and freshly ground pepper, to taste

Serves 2

1 Melt the butter in a saucepan over medium heat. Add the green onions and cook for 1 to 2 minutes. Add the rice and stir to coat.

2 Meanwhile, bring the stock and saffron to a boil. Add $1/2$ cup (125 ml) to the rice and cook over medium heat, stirring, until the stock is absorbed. Add $1/2$ cup (125 ml) more stock and cook, stirring constantly, until almost all the stock is absorbed. Repeat until the rice is tender. For the last $1/2$ cup (125 ml), stir in the stock, cover and let stand off heat.

3 Meanwhile, heat the oil in a frying pan over medium heat. Add the shrimp and cook, turning, until tender, about 3 to 4 minutes. Add the lemon rind, parsley, salt and pepper to taste.

4 Serve the risotto in bowls topped with the shrimp.

Barbecued Shrimp with Toasted Polenta

These lip-smacking good shrimp evoke summertime fun. Serve with ice tea or lemonade.

1 cup (180 g) dried polenta combined with 1
  teaspoon salt and 1 cup (250 ml) water
2 cups (500 ml) boiling water or fish stock
1/4 cup (30 g) grated pecorino or romano cheese
Oil, for cooking
1 1/2 lbs (700 g) fresh jumbo shrimp, peeled
  and deveined
1 bunch arugula (rocket), trimmed and washed
4 ripe tomatoes, quartered
1/3 cup (80 ml) extra virgin olive oil
2 tablespoons balsamic vinegar
3 tablespoons chopped fresh basil
3 cloves garlic, chopped
Freshly ground pepper, to serve

1 Bring the polenta mixture and the water or stock to a boil in a saucepan. Cook over medium heat for 10 minutes, stirring constantly. Reduce heat to very low heat, cover and cook for 15 minutes. Stir in the cheese. Pour into a large greased cake pan and let cool.
2 Using a sharp knife, cut the polenta into 3-in (7.5-cm) squares. Brush with oil and grill or toast until golden brown and toasted.
3 Preheat an oven broiler or grill. Brush the shrimp with oil and grill for 1 to 2 minutes per side, or until tender.
4 To serve, place the polenta squares on plates. Top with some arugula, then the shrimp and tomato. Combine the extra virgin olive oil, vinegar, basil, and garlic and drizzle on top. Sprinkled pepper over the shrimp and serve.

Serves 4

Mussels Steamed in Wine

This classic dish is a great choice when you need to get dinner on the table fast. For a complete meal, serve with a simple green salad. Make sure you have lots of good crusty bread on the side to dip into the delicious sauce.

1 tablespoon oil
2 cloves garlic, minced
$1/_2$ cup (125 ml) dry white wine
$1/_2$ cup (125 ml) fish stock
2 green onions (scallions), chopped
3 tablespoons chopped fresh parsley
2 lbs (1 kg) fresh mussels, scrubbed and
  removed the hairlike strands from the shell
Italian or French bread, to serve

Heat the oil in a large saucepan over medium heat. Add the garlic and stir-fry until fragrant. Add the wine, stock, green onions, parsley and mussels. Cover and bring to a boil. Simmer just until the mussels open, about 2 to 3 minutes. Discard any mussels that do not open. Serve immediately with bread to soak up the broth.

Serves 4–6

Crunchy Calamari Rings

A classic appetizer, tender calamari rings also make a great light lunch when paired with a salad.

2 lbs (1 kg) squid (calamari), cleaned and
  cut into rings
Seasoned all-purpose (plain) flour
2 eggs, beaten
1¹/₂ cups (90 g) breadcrumbs
Oil, for deep-frying
Rémoulade Sauce (page 70), to serve
Lemon wedges, to serve

Serves 4

1 Dust the calamari with the flour, shaking off any excess.
Dip into the egg and then the breadcrumbs, pressing firmly.
Chill for 30 minutes.
2 Heat the oil in deep pan over medium heat until hot. Add the
calamari in batches and cook until crisp and golden, about
1 to 2 minutes each batch. Drain well on paper towels and keep
warm. Serve with the Rémoulade Sauce and lemon wedges.

Note: To make calamari rings crisp and golden, the oil must be at
the correct temperature. To test, sprinkle a few breadcrumbs into
the hot oil; they should start to sizzle immediately but not burn.
Do not cook too many calamari rings at once as this will lower the
temperature of the oil and give soggy results.

Fish Steaks with Citrus and Basil Salsa

The bright acidity of fruit salsas makes them a natural partner with seafood. And being fat-free, they are a great way to bring lots of flavor to a dish without guilt. You can use other firm fish steaks such as swordfish or blue fish with this recipe.

4 tuna, salmon or swordfish steaks, about
  7 oz (200 g) each
Mixed salad greens (optional)
1 tablespoon oil, for frying

Citrus and Basil Salsa
$3/_4$ cup (180 ml) oil
$1/_2$ bunch fresh basil
Juice of 2 limes
1 medium orange
1 hothouse (English) cucumber
1 red onion, finely diced
1 yellow bell pepper, deseeded and finely
  diced
3 tablespoons balsamic vinegar
1 lime, cut into wedges

Serves 4

1 To make the Citrus and Basil Salsa, blend or process the oil with the basil and juice of 1 lime until smooth. Set aside. Peel, deseed and section the orange; dice the sections. Remove the seeds from the cucumber and finely dice the flesh. Combine the orange, cucumber, onion and bell pepper in a small bowl with the rest of the lime juice. Mix well.
2 Prepare the fish steaks by heating the oil in a frying pan and searing the steaks for 1 minute on each side.
3 Arrange each steak on a bed of mixed greens (if using) and top with the Citrus and Basil Salsa and drizzle with vinegar. Serve with the lime wedges.

Notes:
1. This simple dish goes very well served with steamed new potatoes. It is recommended that the fish be only lightly cooked, so that it is still pink in the middle.
2. Grapefruit is a great alternative to orange, but if you use it, leave out the lime juice. For a slightly sweeter salsa, use roasted bell pepper.

Oriental Fish with Cilantro Rice

In this tempting recipe, ginger, soy sauce and fresh coriander are combined in a slightly sweet sauce.

2 cups (400 g) uncooked long-grain rice
3¹/₂ cups (825 ml) water
2 tablespoons chopped coriander leaves
  (cilantro)
1¹/₂ lbs (700 g) fish fillets
3 tablespoons oil
1 small onion, finely chopped
6 green onions (scallions), sliced
1 tablespoon grated fresh ginger
¹/₄ cup (60 ml) soy sauce
2 teaspoons brown sugar
¹/₂ cup (125 ml) fish stock

Serves 4

1 Rinse the rice in a strainer under cold water until the water runs clear. Combine the rice and water in a heavy-based saucepan and bring to a boil, stirring. Reduce the heat, cover tightly and simmer gently for 12 minutes. Remove from the heat and let stand, covered, for 10 minutes. Fluff the rice with a fork, stirring in the coriander leaves (cilantro).
2 Cut the fish into large chunks. Heat the oil in a large frying pan or wok over medium-high heat. Add the fish and cook, turning occasionally, until lightly browned on all sides. Remove from the pan.
3 Add the onion and green onions to the pan and stir-fry for 1 minute. Add the rest of the ingredients and bring to a boil. Return the fish to the pan, cover and simmer for 5 minutes.
4 Serve the rice topped with the fish pieces and drizzled with sauce.

Baked Mediterranean-Style Fish

In this easy recipe, the flavors of lemon, oregano and black olives bring the Mediterranean to your table.

4 fresh fish fillets
4 teaspoons oil
2 ripe tomatoes, sliced
8 pitted black olives, roughly chopped
2 tablespoon chopped parsley
1 tablespoon chopped fresh oregano
2 cloves garlic, crushed
4 teaspoons grated lemon rind
4 teaspoons lemon juice
4 pieces greased aluminum foil, big enough
    to hold the fish and other ingredients

Serves 4

1 Preheat oven to 350°F (180°C).
2 Divide the ingredients equally into 4 portions. Place a piece of fish on the middle of each sheet of aluminum foil. Spread the fish with oil, then top with the tomatoes. Sprinkle the remaining ingredients on top.
3 Fold the two longest ends of the foil over the fish so that they meet in the middle. Fold the edges together so that the packet is tightly sealed. Fold the other sides of the foil.
4 Place the parcels on a baking sheet with the folded edges up so that the juices do not run out. Bake in the oven for about 10–12 minutes, depending on thickness. Thicker pieces will take longer to cook.
5 Remove the fish from the foil and serve with couscous, rice or steamed potatoes.

Quick Fish and Chips

This traditional British dish is most often served with malt vinegar, though tartar sauce or simply a squeeze of fresh lemon is also a good choice. A flour-based batter is traditional, though some variations use a breadcrumb coating. The carbon dioxide in the mineral water (or club soda) gives a lighter texture to the batter.

1 egg
1 cup (250 ml) chilled mineral water or club
 soda (soda water)
1 cup (300 g) all-purpose (plain) flour
1 1/2 lbs (700 g) fresh or frozen fish fillets
 (e.g. bream, snapper, halibut, perch, cod)
Oil, for deep-frying
Lemon wedges and parsley sprigs, to serve
Malt vinegar and tartar sauce, to serve

Serves 4

1 To make the batter, place the egg and water in a bowl and, using a whisk, stir to combine. Sift the flour into the egg mixture and whisk lightly until just blended (batter should be slightly lumpy).
2 Set oven temperature to 300°F (150°C). Cut the fish into thick strips and pat thoroughly dry with paper towels. Line a baking sheet with paper towels.
3 Pour the oil into a large, heavy-based saucepan to a depth of 4 in (10 cm) and heat slowly to 350°F (180°C). Test the oil by frying a cube of bread in the oil—it should brown in 20 to 30 seconds.
4 Using tongs, dip the fish pieces, three at a time, into the batter. Gently drain off any excess. Carefully lower the fish pieces into the hot oil and deep-fry in batches, turning once, for 3 to 5 minutes, or until golden brown and crisp. Use a slotted spoon to lift out the cooked pieces. Drain in a single layer on lined baking sheet.
5 Keep the fish warm in the oven while frying the remaining pieces. Scoop out any floating pieces of batter from the oil between batches.
6 Serve with oven baked potato wedges and lemon, parsley, vinegar and tartar sauce as desired.

Notes:
1. To prevent boiling over, never fill a saucepan with oil more than half-full and never use a lid when deep-frying.
2. For best results, cook foods in small batches so as not to crowd the pan.
3. Allow the oil to return to cooking temperature between each batch. If the oil begins to smoke, the temperature is too high.

Pan-fried Fish with Lemon and Capers

This delicious recipe, featuring lemon, butter and capers, is a simplified version of the famous Sole à la Grenobloise.

1 tablespoon butter
1 teaspoon oil
2 firm fresh fish fillets, such as sole or
 snapper
2 teaspoons grated lemon rind
Juice of $1/_2$ lemon
1 clove garlic, minced
2 teaspoons drained capers
1 tablespoon chopped fresh parsley
Salt and freshly ground pepper, to taste

Serves 2

1 Melt the butter with the oil in a frying pan over medium heat. Add the fish fillets and cook for 2 to 3 minutes on one side.
2 Turn the fish and sprinkle with the remaining ingredients. Cook for 3 minutes, or until just opaque. Serve immediately.

Note: Simple accompaniments are all that's needed—steamed or roasted new potatoes and green salad or steamed spinach. To make crisp baked potatoes for two, preheat oven to 400°F (200°C). Halve the potatoes and brush the cut sides with oil. Arrange on a baking sheet, cut side up. Sprinkle with salt and bake until crisp and golden, about 30 minutes.

Seared Tuna Steaks with Mexican Salsa

In this recipe, a flavorful and zesty salsa transforms ordinary grilled tuna into something special and festive.

2 fresh tuna steaks
1 tablespoon oil
Juice of 1 lime
Salt and freshly ground pepper, to taste

Mexican Salsa
1 large ripe tomato, finely diced
1 small red onion, chopped
1 ripe avocado, peeled, pitted and finely diced
1 red finger-length chili pepper
$^1/_4$ cup (10 g) chopped coriander leaves
$^1/_2$ small red bell pepper, finely diced
2 tablespoons olive oil
Salt and freshly ground pepper, to taste

1 Brush the tuna steaks with oil. Heat an oven broiler or frying pan and sear the tuna over high heat, 2 to 3 minutes on each side, depending on how rare you want it. Test by gently cutting into the middle.
2 To make the Mexican Salsa, deseed and finely chop the red chili pepper. Combine all the ingredients together in a bowl and set aside.
3 Squeeze the lime juice over the tuna steaks and season with salt and pepper. Serve with the Salsa and lime wedges.

Serves 2

Quick Banana and Raspberry Soufflé

This elegant dessert is surprisingly easy to make. If fresh raspberries aren't available, frozen ones can be used.

2 ripe bananas
1 tablespoon lemon juice
4 egg whites
$^1/_4$ cup (30 g) confectioner's (icing) sugar
1 cup (150 g) fresh or frozen raspberries
Confectioner's (icing) sugar, to dust

Serves 4

1 Preheat oven to 450°F (230°C). Lightly grease four cupcake molds with butter or oil.
2 Mash the bananas and lemon juice in a bowl with a fork until well combined, with no large lumps.
3 Beat the egg whites in a large bowl with an electric mixer until soft peaks form. Gradually add the sugar and continue beating until the sugar is completely dissolved and stiff peaks form.
4 Gently fold the egg whites into the banana mixture, then gently fold in the fresh or frozen raspberries. Spoon the mixture into the cupcake molds and arrange on a baking sheet. Bake for 15 minutes, or until puffed and browned. Finish with light dusting of icing sugar and serve immediately.

Easy Lime and Blueberry Crème Brûlée

Crème Brûlée is famous for its crunchy sugary top and the ultra smooth creamy custard beneath.

2 cups (500 ml) whipping cream
1 teaspoon vanilla extract
Finely grated rind of 1 lime
5 egg yolks
Scant $1/_2$ cup (100 g) sugar
1 cup (125 g) fresh or frozen blueberries

Serves 4

1 Preheat oven to 400°F (200°C). Bring the cream just to a boil in a saucepan. Remove from the heat and stir in the vanilla extract and lime rind. Cover and allow the flavors to infuse for 5 minutes.
2 Beat the egg yolks with $3/4$ of the sugar until slightly thickened. Slowly stir in the hot cream, blending well. Divide the blueberries among four heatproof bowls and pour the custard on top.
3 Arrange the bowls in a pan of hot water—the hot water should reach at least halfway up the sides of the bowls. Bake until a skin forms on the surface of the custard, 15 to 20 minutes. Let cool, then chill.
4 To serve, sprinkle each crème brûlée with a little sugar and broil under an oven broiler as close to heat as possible until the sugar melts and caramelizes, about 2 minutes. Serve immediately.

Cinnamon Crumble Banana Cups

With its granola-like topping, this Carribean-inspired dessert could almost double for a rich breakfast treat. But with the additional of dark rum, this exotic sweet rightly holds its place in the canon of delicious post-supper desserts.

1 orange
6 ripe bananas
$1/_2$ cup (90 g) brown sugar, firmly packed
6 tablespoons unsalted butter
6 tablespoons dark rum
$1/_2$ cup (30 g) fresh breadcrumbs (see note)
3 tablespoons rolled oats
$1/_2$ teaspoon ground cinnamon
Whipped cream, to serve
$3/_4$ cup (90 g) chopped toasted pecans (see note), to serve

Serves 4

1 Preheat oven to 400°F (200°C). Finely grate 1 teaspoon of the rind and squeeze 6 tablespoons juice from the orange. Slice the bananas.

2 Place $1/_2$ of the sugar, 2 tablespoons of the butter and 3 tablespoons of the rum in a large frying pan. Cook over medium heat, stirring frequently, until the sugar dissolves and the mixture begins to bubble. Stir in the bananas and toss until evenly coated. Remove from the heat.

3 Divide half of the banana mixture among four heatproof cups.

4 Sprinkle each cup with 1 tablespoon of the breadcrumbs. Top with the remaining banana mixture. Spoon the orange juice over each cup.

5 Combine the remaining breadcrumbs, sugar and butter with the oats, orange rind and cinnamon, blending with your fingertips until the mixture resembles coarse crumbs. Sprinkle the mixture over the bananas.

6 Bake the cups until the topping is crisp and golden, about 15 minutes. Serve warm, topped with whipped cream and chopped pecans.

Notes:
1. To make fresh breadcrumbs, process fresh crustless white bread in a blender or food processor until fine crumbs form.
2. When cooking rum mixture, be sure the heat is not too high or the rum will evaporate very quickly, or could even ignite—and this is not a flambé!
3. Toast the pecans by placing them in a frying pan over medium heat, and fry until lightly browned, stirring constantly, for 3–4 minutes. Be careful not to burn.

Poached Peaches with Sweet Ricotta Cream

This recipe conjures up the light fruit desserts served in Italian homes and cafes lining piazzas. Be sure to use in-season ripe peaches.

2 cups (500 ml) water
3/4 cup (150 g) sugar
2 ripe peaches
1/2 cup (125 g) fresh ricotta cheese
2 tablespoons whipping cream
1 tablespoon brown sugar

Serves 2

1 Heat the water and sugar in a saucepan over low heat to dissolve. When it comes to a boil, reduce the heat and add the peaches, and simmer for 15 minutes. Remove the peaches and set aside.
2 Bring the syrup to a boil again and cook until reduced by half, about 5 minutes.
3 Combine the ricotta, cream and brown sugar.
4 Serve the peaches warm with the syrup and ricotta cream mixture.

Note: You can halve the peaches before poaching them to reduce the cooking time to 10 minutes.

Baked Stuffed Apples

Along with being served as a dessert, this American favorite is often served as a side dish with pork.

4 green apples
1 tablespoon golden raisins
1 tablespoon mixed candied fruit
2 tablespoons ground almonds
1 tablespoon maple syrup
1 tablespoon orange juice
$1/_2$ teaspoon ground cloves
1 tablespoon butter
Pinch of ground nutmeg

Serves 4

1 Preheat oven to 400°F (200°C). Carefully core the apples using an apple corer or small knife. Lightly grease a baking dish with oil or butter and arrange the apples on it.
2 Combine the raisins, candied fruit, almonds, maple syrup, orange juice and cloves in a small bowl and mix well. Press the mixture into the apples; don't worry if the filling overflows slightly. Rub the butter around the tops of the apples and sprinkle lightly with nutmeg.
3 Bake for 20 minutes or until the apple skins are shiny and about to burst.

Note: This dessert is delicious hot or cold, so make a few extra for the next day and serve with a generous portion of thick whipped cream. If serving them hot, let them stand for 5 minutes first after taking them out of the oven to allow the flavors to infuse.

Fruit Poached in Sweet Red Wine

This elegant dessert will satisfy your fruit cravings in the dead of winter.

1 cup (250 ml) red wine
$^1/_2$ cup (100 g) sugar
$^1/_2$ cup (125 ml) water
1 pear, peeled, halved, cored and cut into
   eight wedges
1 cinnamon stick
2 cardamom pods, crushed
Grated rind of $^1/_2$ orange
8 prunes
Mascarpone or whipping cream, to serve
Wafer cookies or biscotti (optional)

1 Combine the wine, sugar and water in a saucepan and stir over low heat to dissolve the sugar. Bring to a boil and reduce the heat to a steady simmer.

2 Add the pears, spices and orange rind and simmer for 10 minutes. Add the prunes and cook until the prunes are tender and plump, 3 to 4 more minutes. Remove the fruit with a slotted spoon and bring the liquid back to a boil. Boil until reduced by half, 3 to 4 minutes.

3 Pour the syrup over the pears and prunes. Serve warm with mascarpone and cookies.

Serves 2

Fresh Summer Fruit Salad

If a fruit isn't in season, simply substitute another fruit. Choose fruits with a mix of colors and textures.

1 grapefruit (pink if in season)
$^1/_2$ cup (125 ml) apricot nectar
$^1/_2$ teaspoon ground ginger
4 cups (600 g) sliced watermelon
2 large nectarines, pitted and cut into wedges
2 cups (300 g) fresh apricots, pitted and cut into wedges
1 basket strawberries
$^1/_3$ cup (80 ml) whipped cream, to serve
2 teaspoons maple syrup
2 teaspoons chopped fresh mint leaves

Serves 6–8

1 Cut one grapefruit in half and squeeze out the juice. Remove the peel and pith from the other grapefruit and cut the fruit into segments.
2 Combine the grapefruit juice, nectar and ginger in a large bowl and mix well.
3 Remove the rind from the watermelon and cut into 1-in (2.5-cm) chunks. Stem and halve the strawberries.
4 Add the fruit to the juice mixture and toss gently to mix well.
5 Combine the cream and maple syrup in a bowl and beat with an electric beater until soft peaks form. Stir in the mint leaves and chill, if possible.
6 Top the fruit with dollop of the whipped cream and mint leaves and serve immediately.

Published by Periplus Editions, Ltd., with editorial offices
at 61 Tai Seng Avenue, #02-12, Singapore 534167.

Copyright © 2008 Lansdowne Publishing Pty. Limited
Recipe contributors: Myles Beaufort, Nicole Gaunt, Suzie
Smith, Kirsten Tilgals and Linda Venturoni-Wilson

Hardcover ISBN 978-0-/946-5037-7

Distributed by
USA
Tuttle Publishing, 364 Innovation Drive,
North Clarendon, VT 05759-9436.
Tel: (802) 773-8930 Fax: (802) 773-6993
info@tuttlepublishing.com
www.tuttlepublishing.com

Asia Pacific
Berkeley Books Pte Ltd.
61 Tai Seng Avenue
#02-12, Singapore 534167.
Tel: (65) 6280-1330 Fax: (65) 6280-6290
inquiries@periplus.com.sg
www.periplus.com

Printed in Singapore
10 09 08   5 4 3 2 1